CHRISTOLOGY
IN PAUL
AND JOHN

Proclamation Commentaries

Christology in Paul and John,
Robin Scroggs

Jesus Christ in Matthew, Mark, and Luke,
Jack Dean Kingsbury

John, D. Moody Smith
(Second Edition, Revised and Enlarged)

Luke, Frederick W. Danker
(Second Edition, Revised and Enlarged)

Mark, Paul J. Achtemeier
(Second Edition, Revised and Enlarged)

Matthew, Jack Dean Kingsbury
(Second Edition, Revised and Enlarged)

Paul and His Letters, Leander E. Keck

PROCLAMATION COMMENTARIES

Gerhard Krodel, *Editor*

The Reality and Revelation of God

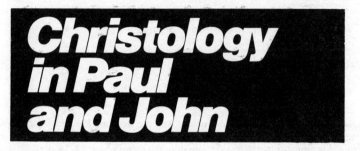

Christology in Paul and John

Robin Scroggs

FORTRESS PRESS   PHILADELPHIA

COPYRIGHT © 1988 BY FORTRESS PRESS

Library of Congress Cataloging-in-Publication Data
Scroggs, Robin.
    Christology in Paul and John: the reality and revelation of God.
    (Proclamation commentaries)
    Bibliography: p.
    Includes index.
    1. Jesus Christ—Person and offices—Biblical teaching. 2. Bible.
N.T. John—Theology. 3. Bible. N.T. Epistles of Paul—Theology.
I. Title. II. Series.
BT198.S373 1988   232'.09'015—dc 19   87-20732
ISBN 0-8006-0599-3

3208F87 Printed in the United States of America 1-599

To
MARILEE
for her courage
and her care

CONTENTS

PREFACE

In my years as a teacher of lay people, ministers, and students preparing for the ministry, I have encountered greater perplexity and sense of mystification about the basic issues of Christology than about any other theological topic. No one seems to know what to do with Jesus Christ! He is faintly honored as an ethical teacher, is said in some vague way to relate us to God, and is extolled as a model for humanity to follow. But few seem to know what any of this means, and I often have the feeling that church people would be just as happy to talk about God and leave Jesus completely on the sideline (where indeed he seems to be most of the time). Even those who delight in reciting the "correct" formulas speak uneasily when asked to explain what they mean by the formulas.

This uncertainty about the meaning of Jesus Christ intensifies when one tries to deal with the texts of Paul and the Gospel of John. The Jesus of Matthew, Mark, and Luke (the Synoptics) is at least a human accessible to "touch" and "sight." The Jesus of the Gospel of John fades into divinity, while in the kerygmatic Christ of Paul the earthly Jesus seems to pull a successful disappearing act. I still remember one minister telling me that he often preached from the Synoptic Gospels but never from Paul!

Can anything be done to make possible a renewed christological vision in the church? Or will Christianity—at least the Protestant denominations with which I am most familiar—continue to live out of a covert Unitarianism? Perhaps a fresh listening to the early founders of the whole christological enterprise—in our case, Paul and John—might help us hear again reverberations we have rarely resonated to. At least for them reflection on the meaning of Jesus Christ was a task they could not avoid. Could not avoid because for them their lives depended on the act of God in Christ. To explain that dependence was a burning prod in their theological gut. "Woe to me if I do not preach the gospel."

Perhaps this concern of mine will explain the pages that follow. I hope I have written a scholarly respectable book. But I hope I have written more than that. I begin with the assumption that believers today are not convinced that Christology is essential to their faith. I uncover, as best I can, the deep dynamic of the christological language and structure of Paul and John, to show why as well as what. In the final chapter I try to show how *both* Christologies show striking fundamental similarities: through the revelation in Christ Paul and John have come to experience the reality of God in a way radically different from all their previous perspectives. To follow these seminal thinkers in their driven pursuit has been for me not only meaningful but exciting, and even good fun. I would like to think I have communicated to the reader something of those pleasures as well.

The officers of Union Theological Seminary in New York graciously granted me a sabbatical at the beginning of my tenure there. This gift of time made the creation of this book not only easier but even a pleasurable experience. Several of my colleagues have read portions of the manuscript and given good advice: Raymond Brown, Louis Martyn, and Peter Van Ness. I stand in their debt. To friend, Judy Wren Brinkworth, who has read all of the pages with the critical eye of a nonspecialist who is not fooled by jargon, I offer especial thanks. John A. Hollar of Fortress Press has shown his customary insightful care for both manuscript and author. In the final analysis, of course, I have had to make my own decisions.

ROBIN SCROGGS
Union Theological Seminary
New York

CHAPTER ONE

THE COMPULSION TO THINK ABOUT JESUS CHRIST

Why?

The first question is why? Why bother to think about Jesus Christ? To use the technical term, why do people do Christology? That word itself—Christology—sticks in one's throat and feels so abstruse. But, like all jargon terms, it is not so threatening once we know what it purports to be about. We can simply define Christology as thinking about Jesus Christ. But why should we?

An immediate response is that Jesus Christ is important for people who believe in him. But I can believe without having to think, without having to analyze—or can I? Can I put my trust in someone about whom I know little or nothing, or whose promises to me I do not understand? Dare I risk my life with someone whom I profess to love and who seems to love me, without having some confidence that I know that person? We think about Jesus Christ precisely because he is important to us.

Indeed we are compelled to think about him. It is a compulsion that comes before reason, that evolves from the depths of our being and is ultimately the source of our becoming thinking believers. Anybody can learn an abstract system of thought and repeat it. That system does not, however, necessarily mean anything to the personal life of the learner. Just so, theological and christological systems can be memorized and spewed out as clichés. However perfect and intellectually "correct" they may be, they are not thereby a reflection of what the human individual wants and needs to say. There may be no contact with the experience of the individual.

In an important way such use of theology is misuse, and that is because at their hearts theology and Christology should be reflections on the experience of the believer. Unless the believer has experienced something in the depths of her being, she has nothing to say. She has nothing to think about. There are other definitions of theology, but I do not think anyone will deny a necessary connection between what is spoken and some depth experience of the speaker, an experience the believer takes to be an encounter with the divine.[1]

Because of this encounter, the believer is compelled to attempt to describe for himself and for others its meaning and source. There is no option but to "do Christology." The Christian mystics, for example, are notorious for coming from a peak experience, saying that it is impossible to describe it—and then writing fifty pages trying to do just what they know they cannot.

Without some experience, however unmystical it may be, thinking about Jesus will remain abstract and probably abstruse. With it, the believer will want to attempt to describe as clearly and coherently as possible the meaning and source of what has happened to her. But how does one interpret one's own feelings and perceptions? Mature people know that experiences are tricky and can deceive.

Casual, individualistic thinking will not do. Our thinking must be sifted and systematic. This is so because our relation to Jesus Christ is in part mediated through the knowledge and reflection of Christian tradition. While the believer may wish to affirm a direct relationship with Jesus Christ, it is still true that this relationship is informed by what others have experienced and thought. A singular and unique relationship might be suspect (schizophrenic?).

The believer needs to sift through the many ways other people have felt it important to talk about Jesus Christ. The believer needs, further, to systematize as best as possible what is sifted, to come to a coherent view. Without some sort of basic coherence our understanding of Jesus Christ, and of the God who acts through this person, remains unstable and flimsy. That is why a study of Christology is essential for the believer with even the most deeply felt experience. To know how Paul and the author of John interpreted their encounters with Jesus Christ helps us in our own quest for the meaning of our lives as believers.

How?

The second question is how does one go about "doing Christology"? Specifically I want to ask: *How did the earliest believers begin to think about Jesus Christ?* Today we have the resources of two thousand years of theologians. At the beginning, believers were forced to think about something new to their experience without that benefit. What words, what categories were at their disposal? And how did they go about choosing, from what was at their disposal, what best expressed what had happened to them? To put it succinctly, how did they describe something new (at least for them) with old language? To answer this way of putting the question, we need to talk about building blocks and breakthroughs.

Building Blocks

Our language—our entire way of understanding and expressing ourselves and our world in words, syntax, and concepts—is both given and acquired. We are given a particular culture and receive unselfconsciously the ways of thinking and speaking of that culture.[2] We share this language with all others in the same culture. In a real way it is the world we believe to be true and desirable.

As we grow up we acquire more specific forms of language. We become knowledgeable about certain fields—biology, plumbing, physics, computers, cooking, or philosophy, for instance. With this knowledge we learn a specific language, a "language field." Our acquired language fields give us the freedom to talk easily with others who have that same language field. As a sometime musician I can speak with another musician using the jargon of musical structure, developments in tonality, and so forth.

At the same time the fact—obvious and painful—that I do not have access to other language fields excludes me from many conversations. I am sure I am not alone in experiencing frustration at being forced to listen to a conversation the technical language of which keeps me from any understanding of what is being said. Language fields both open and close doors.

Thus when we are compelled to speak about a new reality in our lives, we inevitably begin with language fields that are "old," that is, with which we are acquainted. We attempt to express something new with something old. The old we pick will be a language field comfortable to us and to some others, but not to all. If we use the language of lawyers, for example, or medical doctors, we cannot expect to be understood by everyone. This is the obvious reason why first-century Christology is not immediately transparent to our twentieth-century understanding—it uses building blocks of its own time and culture, language fields which are, at least to a certain extent, foreign to our own.

Imagine, for example, the invention of a Christology in our decades built on the building block of sports culture. What would one say about Jesus Christ? That he was a wise coach? That he hit home runs? That he was a leader of his team? Or (to refer to the language of the cross), that he came to bat in the bottom of the ninth and struck out? The possibilities of the use of this language field are immense and intriguing. One thing is clear: A Christology built on these metaphors would certainly seem different from that of a Paul or a John.

But would it really be saying something different? That would depend, would it not, on whether the experience lying behind the language was the same or different from those behind the language of a Paul or a John? At the same time, it is obvious that to grasp what is being pointed to by any language field requires an understanding of terms, idioms, and so forth. To someone who knew nothing about baseball, for example, to say that Jesus either "drove in the winning run" or "struck out" would not communicate any better than Paul's language of justification does to most people today.

Breakthroughs

Language, however, does not sit still, especially under the pressure of intense experiences. While the mystic may use the old language, he or she is quite aware it is inadequate. Thus the use of the old language field is volatile and unstable. Attempts are inevitably made to change the way the language is used, to infuse old words with new meanings, to create neologisms, sometimes even to develop a new syntax. If the experience persists and a community grows which continues to share that experience, there comes such a breakthrough in language that a new language field may in effect be created. To an outsider, even one who was intimately acquainted with the terms, the old–new language may be at best baffling and at worst offensive (e.g., "That's *not* what that word is supposed to mean!").

This forging of a new language field out of an old one we can legitimately call a breakthrough. When we identify such a breakthrough we can know with assurance that a vital new experience is seething under the lava flow of words and sentences. As we will see, Paul's language field was the legal world of first–century Judaism. He picked up that field and used it—but in significantly unusual ways. Hence the believer, Paul, while sharing a language field with his Pharisaic colleagues—or former colleagues— created a language different enough to arouse the wrath of those colleagues. Paul's experience of the Christ forced him to a breakthrough in a language field with which he had been very comfortable in the past.

One additional complexity needs to be noted. Most people, confronted with the impossibility of expressing a new experience with old words, will try as many different language fields as they have at their disposal. Our hypothetical sports enthusiast, for example, may find that sports imagery does not communicate in a specific situation, so he turns to culinary language. Part of the breakthrough then will involve putting together different language fields into what may seem from the outside like a series of hashed metaphors.

If this process goes on long enough, a genuinely new language field may emerge, with its component parts having originated in several different language fields but now integrated into a new structure, each part now playing a role within the total system and different from that in its previous "location." By this time the primal, "given" language has also been reworked, because the experience has forced a change of worlds.

One can say that classical Christology is just such a new language world developed out of many building blocks from previous language fields. Here we have a profusion of biblical language mixed with classical and postclassical Greek philosophic concepts. The later we move through the history of christological thinking, the more layers we have to add—for example, the theory of satisfaction from the social structure of medieval feudalism. When we look at the Christologies of Paul and the Gospel of John, however, we find ourselves at the very beginning of the process. This makes our task simpler.

Christology as Metaphor

All we have said above points to a simple but, perhaps for some, alarming conclusion: thinking about Jesus Christ inevitably involves one in thinking metaphorically. Indeed, it can be claimed that all theology is metaphor and inevitably so. What do I mean?

Already the author of John seems to be aware of what the later mystics knew well: God is transcendent but words are immanent, that is, they belong to this world, this very finite, imperfect society. Our words are creations of that finite world. To talk about God or God's acts, hence Christology, is to involve one in the use of the immanent to describe the transcendent. Thus words are not—cannot be—literal significations of God or God's acts.

If we understand what this means, it should not be frightening. A metaphor, to abide by the terms we have already suggested, is the use of a word or concept from one language system to point to a reality not in that system. This nonliteral quality is even more the case in theological language. If all language systems are immanent, then the realm of the divine, the transcendent, *cannot possess a language system of its own.* Thus the transcendent can only be expressed through metaphor.

Reflection on our hypothetical use of sports language makes this clear. Whether one describes Jesus Christ as "hitting a home run" or as "striking out," the speaker clearly does not mean this in some literal fashion. Jesus never played baseball! The speaker is, rather, trying to say something about the significance of what God has done in Jesus Christ through a language field which is familiar to the speaker and those to whom he wishes to communicate. What he is expressing is an understanding of God's transcendent act, but how he does it is through a finite language system. Just so, when

Paul the lawyer uses the concept of justification, he is using a language field familiar to him to express the literally unutterable work of God. When the author of John describes Jesus Christ as the descending–ascending Son of man, he is speaking equally metaphorically.

The task of understanding a christological language field is twofold. First, we have to analyze as carefully as possible the field from which the metaphor is taken—to get inside the whole linguistic world of the speaker. Second, we must try to discover the experience of God's transcendent act through Christ, which the speaker is bringing to expression through the use of the metaphor. That means we are seeking to understand the change, the transformation in the speaker's experience, from a situation before the encounter with Jesus Christ to that which has been brought about as a result of the encounter.

The Person and the Work
of Jesus Christ

The interpreter is always confronted with the task of organizing his or her presentation and making evaluative decisions about priorities. Theologians have traditionally and conveniently divided the discussion of Christology into two categories: *the person and the work of Jesus Christ.*

In postbiblical terms, reflections about the person of Jesus Christ consider his "nature," both divinity and humanity. Since biblical thought does not know the concept of "nature" as a characteristic of the divine, our discussion of Paul and John cannot deal with "nature" as this category was developed in later theology.[3] It is, however, customary to speak about the person of Jesus Christ in terms of the titles ascribed to him by the various biblical authors. Thus reflection is necessitated on terms such as Messiah, Son of God, Son of man, and Savior. What is the status of Jesus Christ pointed to by such titles and what is the relationship with God implied?

Reflection on the work of Jesus Christ considers what God has done through Jesus Christ for world, human society, and the individual. Here terms such as justification, redemption, salvation, or notions such as God sending His son so that all who believe in him might have eternal life are discussed.

For New Testament thought I think it can be persuasively argued that this latter category is primary.[4] What God *has done* is the focus of excitement and joy. The terms used to describe the status of Jesus Christ are secondary because they are inferential from the work of Christ. That is, it is on the basis of a conviction of what God *has done* that the inference is drawn as to who Jesus Christ must be.[5] Otherwise the terms are easily reduced to slogans isolated from the basic experiential reality.

For this reason, compelling to me, I will focus in the following chapters on what Paul and the author of John have to say about *the act of God* in Jesus Christ. Titles are certainly important and we will reflect upon the ones used by our authors. In John's system, titles are indeed an important means by which he communicates the meaning of God's act. Nevertheless, even for the evangelist the titles serve the more fundamental purpose.

Christology and the Theological System

The reader should keep in mind a second set of decisions any author on our topic must make. I have just implied that Paul and John have created theological systems. Neither, of course, was a systematic theologian.[6] Yet they have integrated in an amazing way, given their place at the beginning point, all of the realities of their Christian experience and their understanding of the world. Creation, fall, human existence, the work of the Spirit, and the understanding of God are all reflected upon by our authors, in some instances explicitly, in some more tangentially. These components all interlock. That is, what one says about one of them is influenced by what one thinks about others and, in turn, informs what one thinks about the others.

How, then, can one reflect on Christology without involving some or even all of the other components? Strictly speaking one cannot. To speak about Jesus Christ clearly involves a reinterpretation of an author's previous understanding of God. To speak about Jesus Christ necessitates reflection on the work of the Spirit, which, especially in John, is inseparably linked with God's act in Jesus Christ. My task, however, is not to write a book about theology but about a specific component of that, namely Christology. How can this be done?

I will not pretend it is easy or without extreme frustration at times, both to author and reader. I can only hope to hold the tension in balance, focusing on Christology and trying to point to the other components only when they interlock in central fashion.

Conclusion

For those who believe—or are struggling to believe—in Jesus Christ, this book will hopefully prove more than just an intellectual venture. To deal with what God has done in Jesus Christ is to deal with the deepest levels of ourselves. The more we fathom new possibilities for our selfhood and our world, the more we grasp what God has done in Jesus Christ. The converse is equally true.

For those who read with interest but without struggle for commitment, this book will hopefully prove an exciting intellectual venture. We deal here with seminal thinkers at the beginning of a significant movement in human history. What they have written has certainly influenced the direction of Western civilization. We may not agree that they are ultimately correct, but it is hard to deny them a stimulating and profound originality.

THE CHRISTOLOGY OF PAUL

CHAPTER TWO

GOD'S ACT OF RESTORATION: JUSTIFICATION BY GRACE

Although one should not try to separate Paul the historical person from his writings, it is impossible here to say much about the life of the apostle. Fortunately, adequate accounts of his life are available.[1] For our purposes we have to be content with the following essentials.

Paul was a later contemporary of Jesus; his missionary career spanned the years from the mid 30s to the late 50s or early 60s of the first century. He was born and raised a Diaspora Jew: he was bicultural, knowing Greek as well as Hebrew, and was almost certainly influenced by popular Greek culture.[2] He called himself a Pharisee (Phil. 3:5), and according to Acts 22:3 (a passage the historicity of which is disputed by some), was educated under Gamaliel I, a leading Palestinian Pharisee. Whether this is a fact or not, Paul's writings make it abundantly clear that he had advanced training in Pharisaic law and hermeneutic. Paul was, it is fair to say, a lawyer, and it is this background that often strongly influences both the form and the style of his thinking and writing.

After Paul felt called to follow Jesus, he joined other similarly committed followers—some were Jews as informed by Greek culture as he was; some were Gentiles. The new apostle could not help but be influenced by the form of the Christologies already being formed in these communities. Thus Paul's mature christological language field is indebted to the building blocks of two cultures.

Nor is is possible here to discuss, much less debate, the arguments that revolve around the issue of the genuineness of the letters ascribed to Paul in the New Testament. Such discussions can also be found elsewhere. I follow what is regarded in much scholarship today as the sure list of authentic letters: Romans, 1 and 2 Corinthians, Galatians, 1 Thessalonians, Philippians, and Philemon. To arrange these letters in a convincing order of composition is impossible, simply because we do not have enough information to do so. It may be that Romans is the last extant authentic letter.[3]

The above issues, however settled, do not affect the discussion of Paul's Christology in significant fashion. What is crucial is the debate, which has raged for a century, about what counts as the center or the focus of Paul's theology. The most widely known and long–lived claim is one that goes back to Saint Augustine (and before), Martin Luther, and in this century championed by Rudolf Bultmann: Justification by grace through faith is the center. For a number of reasons exception has been taken to this claim, and other perspectives proposed, such as mysticism, covenantal Pharisaism, and apocalypticism.[4] The decision I have reached after many years of struggle with the Pauline texts is that justification is indeed the motif which is the center of Paul's theology—from which center all the other important components of his structure are to be understood. Knowledgeable people will find my interpretation informed heavily by both Bultmann and Ernst Käsemann.[5]

One important final claim must be stated. If justification by grace through faith is the center of Paul's theology, it is thereby the center of his Christology. In fact, it needs to be said pointedly: *The motif of justification is Paul's Christology.*[6] In this motif is to be discovered the heart of what God has done in Christ, as Paul understands that act. Thus to expound Paul's Christology means to place this theme at the center of exposition. All others—including all titles—are secondary and must find their meaning in relationship to that center.[7]

The Need for Restoration

We need to begin very simply. The very earliest gropings for a Christology imply that there was a felt need for such thinking. But what does this mean? At the least it means that thinkers such as Paul thought something out of place in God's cosmos. (All such thinking took place within the overarching structure of belief in God's creation of the world.) What was wrong was expressed differently by different thinkers. For some it was the cosmic-political conception of wrong or evil rulers over this world. For others it was the ethical idea that people were sinners. However thought out, there would have been no lasting Christology without this basic sense that there is something gone amiss in the world that needs righting.

It must be emphatically stated that the thinking is not to be seen as a process of logical reasoning from some insight into what is wrong to an ideal solution which is then pinned on the person of Jesus (or the reverse). In fact it may be—and this seems to have been the case with Paul—that one first has the reality of Jesus Christ thrust unwelcomed upon oneself and through that encounter begins to perceive that something is wrong. As we will see, the greatest problem with the perception of the world about itself is that it does not see that something is wrong. Thus the logical relation spoken of in the text must not be equated with the historical process of the person coming to believe.

Early believers experienced this "righting," this restoration, and developed their thinking about what was amiss in correlation with their emerging Christology. Thus it is helpful and perhaps simplest to begin with the understanding of what Paul thinks the problem of the world is.

The Fall into a False World

Although Paul never uses the word "fall," it is a convenient shorthand to describe a distortion of humanity from God's created goodness. Traditionally one associates the fall with the misdeed of Adam. This was already a popular theme in postbiblical Judaism, and Paul himself introduces this idea in Christianity for the first time, with his statements in 1 Corinthians 15 and Romans 5. The apostle's primary purpose in these passages, however, is to develop a view of Christ as the counterfoil to Adam. The "falling away" of humanity is stated but not explained in this topos.[8]

It is rather in Rom. 1:18-32 that Paul most fully develops his understanding of what has gone wrong.[9] Humanity has rejected the true Creator God and has substituted a false, idolatrous reality. The result of this falsification, however, is not just a false theology (false god); it is equally the creation of a false world and a false self. That is, the fall means literally the creation of a world totally different from the one God created. In this sense "world" is a social construct, since we do actually live in the world given us by the society in which we live, a world ultimately created by that society.[10] And, of course, every society thinks its own world is true, ontologically real.

In Rom. 1:18 Paul begins by speaking of people who "suppress the truth." The following verses show that this means suppressing the truth of God's reality. The result of this suppression is that their ability to perceive true reality is destroyed: "Their senseless minds [RSV; Paul writes *kardia,* "heart," but he means the organ of thinking] were darkened" (v. 21). The tragic irony is that people do not know they have created a false world but think instead that the world they live in is true and good and beautiful: "Claiming to be wise, they became fools . . ." (v. 22).

The following verses describe the deformation of the self, individually and corporately, which is the result of the substitution of the false god for the true. In a highly rhetorical section, punctuated by the thrice-repeated "God gave them up," Paul delineates all of the dimensions of the human in its distortion: body (v. 24), emotions (v. 26), mind and conduct (v. 28). Particularly instructive is the phrase in v. 28 which the RSV translates "base mind." The Greek is *adokimos nous. Dokimos* refers to the ability to seek out and know, both the capacity and the success at so doing; with the negating prefix, *a,* the phrase points to a mind incapable of knowing what is true reality.

The "fall" thus means humanity's refusal to remain as creatures under the Creator God, and the subsequent failure to know that this fall has taken place. Humanity lives in a false world with a false self because it no longer knows who God really is, however much it may appeal to him and enshrine him in religion, in cult and ethics. Thus this fallen humanity is not in itself an evil society as defined by worldly standards. Indeed it may be religious and morally upright and proud of its standing with the divine. Resting on its own comprehension, it could not understand when someone like a Paul would declare it to be separated and alienated from the true God. As suggested, the ultimate tragedy of this world is that it does not know its falsity and as a result must brand any proposed alternative world as itself false. Paul, with almost brazen audacity, makes the judgment that all religions, including Judaism (cf. Gal. 4:8–9), are imprisoned in this false world.

Nowhere, however, in this passage in Romans does Paul give us any content: he does not describe who the true God is and who the false, nor does he delineate what sort of falsification is involved in the world created by humanity. In fact the usual words Paul uses for sin do not appear at all. What is said to be wrong is simply the refusal to acknowledge the true God. One could even be misled into equating sin with ignorance, except that Paul makes it clear that he is talking about willful ignorance. Thus "sin" is not to be equated with immorality, although Paul believes it can lead to immoral consequences (cf. vv. 24–32). In fact, in Romans 7 (according to the scholarly exegesis I follow concerning this disputed text) Paul writes about sinners who are not in any obvious way sinners at all![11] Since righteousness consists in relationship with God, worshiping a false god inevitably results in a false relationship with the true God. Thus relationship with the false god is being a sinner, no matter how pious are the acts of the person.[12]

God's Act of Restoration

To restore the world to true relationship with herself God must somehow break into this closed circle where humanity, however piously, worships a false god and recreate a people able and willing to acknowledge who she really is. Thus this breakthrough cannot be simply information, a new script from on high. It must be a profoundly transformative act which alters the selfhood of the person, including first of all the cognitive powers (which are always volitionally controlled), and which liberates the person from this false world in which he or she has been living. Hence forgiveness is not a sufficient ending point (no one in the false world knows he or she needs forgiveness for being in that world)—and it is no accident that Paul never uses the term "forgiveness," except when he is quoting Scripture. Something much more is required; for this "much more" Paul chooses the slogan—taken from his legal language system—"justification by grace."

The Meaning of "Justification"

Paul was a lawyer and it is not surprising that he chose a legal term to point to the central meaning for him of God's restorative act. The word (Hebrew: *tsadaq*; Greek: *dikaioō*) denotes the act of the judge when she acquits an accused person. Thus the closest English equivalent term in legal terminology is "acquittal." The antonym is "conviction" or "condemnation." That Paul thinks in this idiom is clear from the elaborate legal metaphor he sets up in Rom. 8:33–34: "Who shall bring charges against the elect of God? It is God who acquits [justifies]. Who is to condemn?"(au. trans.).

Originally the act of justifying is first that of the human judge, who is, indeed, exhorted in Scripture not to acquit the guilty (cf. Exod. 23:7, with God as the model). The act is in this context relational and covenantal, since by the act the accused is restored to full status within the people of God. It is also, or can be, an act of vindication, since the judge in Israel was supposed to seek out the injured party and see that justice was meted out.

God is, however, the ultimate judge, and the term is inevitably "theologized" to point to God's own decisions regarding the people. In this context the nuances of covenant and vindication are important. Second Isaiah is illustrative of the use of "justify" in this larger theological framework.

He who vindicates [*tsadaq*] me is near.
Who will contend with me?
Let us stand up together.
Who is my adversary?
Let him come near to me.
Behold the Lord God helps me;
Who will declare me guilty?
(Isa. 50:8–9)

The LXX can even occasionally translate *hesed,* the Hebrew word which best expresses Yahweh's covenant loyalty, by *dikaiosynē.* Whoever the speaker in the passage of Isaiah quoted above is thought to be (individual or collective), the covenantal context in general in the Hebrew Bible indicates that God's judging activity, either in condemnation or acquittal, is directed toward the people as a totality. The individual participates in the judgment because he or she is a member of that people.

When Israelite theology begins to deal with the future, a context we can call eschatological, a new stage in the development of the theology of justification occurs. Now the people look forward to the future (either as a series of events in history, or as a final, concluding event to end history), to anticipate or to fear God's judgment. Insofar as eschatological thinking foresees that future as an ultimate, climactic end of history, justification becomes an ultimate and final, irreversible decision of God. The criterion of God's decision, however, still seems to be that of covenant loyalty, with the individual a member of the corporate entity.

A further change occurs. Toward the beginning of classical Judaism (a term I use to include all of postbiblical Judaism down through the rabbinic era), the independence of the individual in judgment becomes prominent. No longer is membership in the people sufficient; what the individual does becomes the criterion for God's judgment. We see this emphasis on the individual's responsibility in the thought of John the Baptist, Jesus, and Paul, as well as in *4 Ezra* and the hazy beginnings of rabbinic thought. The first century marks the early flowering of this emphasis, although it never completely replaces the older corporate ideas, even in Paul.

That a person is judged according to merit or deeds, however, does not in and of itself give us the criterion by which the person is to be judged. What gives him or her this merit? What sort of deeds are required? In Pharisaic theology, the specific background of Paul's own thinking, the criterion is fidelity to the Torah with emphasis laid upon the specific commands of the Mosaic law. Whether one follows the law, however interpreted by whatever group, determines one's final judgment.

A person is thus justified or condemned depending upon his or her faithfulness in obedience to the law. Such a bald statement almost caricatures the subtleties and nuances built into the emerging Pharisaic system. No Jew on record ever said one had to fulfill the law perfectly. Emphasis is laid repeatedly upon the possibility and importance of repentance and the presence and priority of God's mercy in judgment. Nevertheless, these are flexibilities built into the structure, nuances which can so easily camouflage the dynamic of the structure itself. While it is not unusual to charge Paul with unfairness in his description of the Pharisaic system as "justification by works of the law,"[13] I think it fair to say in response that Paul is one of those geniuses who can cut through camouflage and lay bare the skeleton of the structure itself. At any rate, *the Judaism Paul describes* as the foil for his own alternative vision can be simply stated: A person is justified or condemned depending upon his or her faithfulness in obedience to the law.

Paul's New Vision of God

This structure, under which Paul lived for so many years and which he now believes to be false, *is false precisely because the apostle perceives the God implied by this structure to be false.* That God is a god who commands and demands, who warns and chastises and who ultimately kills if obedience is not performed.[14] It is this implied god who lies at the basis of the world created by the Pharisaic structure and on which the entire structure, including the understanding of the self rests and depends. Under that god the self is defined in terms of performance, of doing, of justification by works of the law.

Paul has now come to know that God is not like this, not that the apostle thinks to change religion (Paul never converted to something called Christianity!);[15] rather he now believes that Yahweh is not to be defined as he had been taught, and he sees a new face of God as he reads the Torah. It is not that Paul changes gods, or certainly not that God has changed. It is rather that the one, eternal God has been tragically misread and misinterpreted. From his new comprehension of God, Paul's world becomes different (this is the ultimate effect of his foundational experience on the Damascus road). This radical reinterpretation of God and Torah is visibly present in Romans—in fact that reinterpretation is really the leitmotif of the treatise.[16]

But how does Paul "know" all this? He has come to know it because of the Christ-event. This is the ultimate burden of Paul's Christology and is what drives him to delve as deeply as he does into the meaning of that event. And how does the apostle language this meaning? He does not do it by changing language fields. He remains within his legal terminology but so transforms it that it shocks the sensibilities of those familiar with it.

Justification by Grace

It is not possible to describe and explain the historical processes in Paul's thinking and feeling which led him to his new world. We have no autobiographical writing like Augustine's *Confessions*. We can speculate on the basis of psychological and sociological theories what may have happened. Since we cannot know, however, it is best in this place to leave all such speculation aside. Nor can we, of course, prove that his new world is true and the old false. All that is accessible to us is his description of the event that turned his world upside down, or as he would think, rightside up.

For this is what the act of God in Jesus Christ, as he understands it, has done. God through Jesus Christ has broken into this false world, this world of sin and death and made a new world possible. "If anyone is in Christ, there is the new creation; the old has passed away, behold the new has come" (2 Cor. 5:17, au. trans.). To describe this new reality, Paul feels forced to turn his language "rightside up." Instead of justification by works of law, he now posits justification by grace. His radical revisioning can be described in a series of propositions.

1. Justification is past, not future. In the structure Paul inherited, God's ultimate judgment is future, and one must look either anxiously or confidently to that future for acceptance into eternal life. Paul claims God's judgment to be a past event, centered in the death and resurrection of Jesus Christ (Rom. 1:17–18; 3:21; 4:25; 5:1). In his humiliating death is, paradoxically, both concealed and revealed God's final decision for humanity. Both human anxiety and confidence are undermined by this affirmation, because the decision has been reached independently of what a person offers God through his or her life, either by way of achievement or failure.

Paul is not free of ambiguities at this point. He can, indeed, speak about a judgment which is future (e.g., 2 Cor. 5:10). Scholarly frustration on this variance has led to a number of different hypotheses to explain the inconsistency.[17] In my judgment either Paul has not integrated all of his expressions into his new structure or, more likely, he retains the understanding that there are gradations of reward for the believer to be revealed in the future, although the assurance of salvation is entirely secured by the past event (cf. 1 Cor. 3:10–15; 4:5). I know of no passage which states unequivocally that believers will be judged in the future on the basis of their works (not even in Romans 2).

2. *Justification is for all people.* In the inherited structure God decides that some will be justified and others condemned. Paul now believes in a God who justifies all people. "For God imprisoned all people in disobedience that he might have mercy on all" (Rom. 11:32, au. trans.). "For as in Adam all die, so also in Christ shall all be made alive" (1 Cor. 15:22). While some have suggested that Paul is affirming a genuine universalism here (all people will be saved), we should perhaps remain with the more modest judgment that all who have faith (his more usual statement) are justified. At any rate, I think my conclusion is fair: *Paul is affirming a universal gift.* But one must accept the gift in order for the gift to be effective.

3. *Justification is of the impious.* In the inherited structure God was understood to acquit, to accept into the kingdom, only those who deserved it, those who were by whatever criterion "righteous." Thus it was a justification of the deserving. To acquit the sinner, the guilty, was by definition, of course, an act of immorality on the part of the judge, and we have seen how the Hebrew Bible militates against such action. How much greater the immorality if it is the sovereign and righteous God who should justify the impious! For all the emphasis upon the mercy of God in postbiblical Judaism, there are still limits of righteousness which the Jew assumed God set upon his own mercy. The structure if it is to exist must maintain its basic boundaries. And it is this structure which underlies both the relative leniency of some rabbis and the relative rigidity of *4 Ezra.*

At this point Paul breaks the structure in radical fashion. Not only is the act of justification as a past event supremely indifferent about human accomplishment, but also the truth of the matter as Paul sees it is that the past of every human being is that of a sinner, one who is impious. Thus if God were to justify only the righteous, then no one would, could, be acquitted. "For all have sinned and are lacking the glory of God" (Rom. 3:23, au. trans.). Even Abraham, who is held up as the "knight of faith," in Romans 4, is precisely in that context identified as impious (v. 5). We need to recall what Paul means by sin. To be a sinner is not primarily to be someone who performs obvious acts of immorality. In fact, a sinner may observe the highest ethical standards of his society. Paul himself, as a dedicated member of the Pharisees, knew himself to be blameless in his performance of the Torah (Phil. 3:6). To be a sinner means to participate in that false world which calls upon a false god as its criterion for devotion and action. Thus, to be a sinner means to have a false understanding of world and of self. In the context of Pharisaism, as Paul perceived it, to be a sinner was to worship a God who demanded obedience and threatened to kill if that obedience was not forthcoming and to have a self-understanding as one who derived authentic existence from that obedience. Hence one *could* be blameless in performing the law and still be a sinner. Insofar as performance is designed to authenticate and legitimate the self, the performance is false, hence not that kind of being and action that God desires and makes possible in the new, true world.

Has then Paul made God into an immoral actor, a capricious power who by God's actions invalidates any moral structure of humankind? Or is God so weak and impotent that God must forgive and forgive and forgive? A first clue that this is not what Paul intends is what we have already said, that Paul does not talk about God forgiving people. Forgiveness is not enough. God's act of justification is an act of power which transforms, which liberates people from the false world and empowers them to discover that new world in which one can worship the true God and be a true self.[18]

That is, the act of justification, if it is appropriated by a person, enables her to cease being a sinner because it not only reveals the vision of the true world but frees her to enter it. Only God's act of universal justification removes the reality of sin. Forgiveness would remove only the guilt but not sin's power, since the person is still "ruled" by the false world and its values.

4. Grace not works. Everything said up to this point forces one to the inevitable conclusion: Justification as God's act liberating sinners from the false world is an act of pure gift, a total gift. Paul's word is "grace." Luther glossed correctly when he added, "grace alone." It is at this point that we must see Paul's thinking as a radical either-or. Justification cannot be some works and some grace. If it is justification at all, it is a justification by grace.

There are two complementary ways of looking at sheer gift: (1) There is no evil so extreme, so violent, so comprehensive that it excludes one from God's gift. (2) There is no good so extravagant, so magnificent, so dedicated that it earns God's act of acceptance. Despite the evil a person has done, regardless of the good one has done, God gives justification as sheer gift to one and all.

A radical revisioning of God and world is required here. How can a person whose deeds have made him an outcast in the eyes of moral society come to trust that God does indeed accept him and give him the sheer gift of life? How can a person who has spent her life piling up moral deeds in her ledger be willing, be free to trash that list and to know that her relation to God does not depend upon her performance but simply upon God's prior and abounding love? To the extent that both may find it impossible to take the respective steps, it shows that both live in the same world based on a God who demands performance. Thus for Paul both live in the same false world, although one has reacted in rebellion and the other in submission. Dare we say it: Submission is a subtle form of rebellion.[19]

Even if they are told that an alternative world is possible, even if a complete scenario is offered them, the knowledge in and of itself will not produce change. They may be too ingrained in their own world, however unpleasant it may be; they may reject the alternative as too much a fairy tale.

The difficulty in transformation for either person exhibits clearly the fact that one cannot think oneself into a different world. One must be graced. One must be empowered. God's act in Christ, as Paul knows it, is exactly that act which both reveals the new world and empowers—liberates—one to enter it.

In Christ God reveals who God is and what is God's will for the world. God is not one who demands and threatens to kill. God is the gracious God who gives and loves. "If God is for us, who is against us? He who did not spare his own Son but gave him up for us all, will he not also give us all things with him?" (Rom. 8:31–32). God gives life graciously before a person can earn it. God is a Father who really does care and shower good gifts upon God's children. As we will see (chap. 3), this overflowing love which liberates one from the false world is focused for Paul in the paradoxical power of the cross.

But this changes a person's basic self-understanding. No longer is the self defined by doing, by deeds of heroism, beneficence, morality. The self, as the recipient of the gift of life, is now defined in terms of being, a person who knows herself gifted and who knows she does not have to strive aggressively to earn acceptance. To live life as gift is to live in a different world from that of the self defined by the performance principle.

This new understanding of God also changes one's perception of the world. The world is no longer a place where one has to use others to secure one's own status, a collection of people and groups against which one has to defend oneself. Now the world is a community of people who need the love and care the believer now finds it possible to offer. The neighbor becomes real for the first time.

The world now becomes a place where one believes a mutuality of love can be expected. It is now OK to anticipate and desire love in return for love. But since, obviously, only those who also live in the new world can bestow love, only a community of like-minded people can bring into reality the communal dimensions of the true world. For this reason the church is of such crucial importance for Paul: the church is (or is supposed to be!) the new world in its partial realization.

In Christ, according to Paul, God empowers people to leave the false world and enter the true world under the true God. In Christ God liberates people to switch worlds. How does this happen? To this apparently simple question Paul, insofar as I know, has no answer. His simplest response might be, "It just does!" Paul knows this experientially—about himself and about the many others he knows in the church.

He can locate this power as residing in proclamation, the preaching of the cross (1 Cor. 1:17–25). But what gives the proclamation such power? Perhaps rather tautologically, Paul asserts that the proclamation has such power because it is the power of God (1 Cor. 1:24).

Can more be said? Paul does not, I am afraid, help us. To say more is possible, but it must remain speculation. Such speculation, in my judgment, is best informed by psychology and sociology of knowledge. Somehow the proclamation—the content of which is the vision of the true world under the true God—penetrates through the level of intellectual, self-conscious construction of world and dislodges the primordially ingested world based on the false god. It engages the person at the very roots of perception such that it disturbs preconscious structures and enables the new vision to be formed in place of the old. In psychological language, a new identification with Father as truly loving and giving takes the place of the old father known preconsciously as autocratic and threatening.

However we may explore the various avenues opened up to us today by modern fields of inquiry, Paul knows the power of the proclamation of God's act in Christ, knows that it happens within the individual and takes reality, however precariously, in the community of believers. This is the heart of Paul's Christology. There is, however, one further step that Paul invites us to make. We must come to understand the "theology of the cross."

CHAPTER THREE

THE CROSS: THE REVELATION OF THE TRUE WORLD

"Paul's theology is a theology of the cross." This statement has become a virtual slogan in Pauline scholarship today, whether that scholarship is liberal or conservative. The problem here is not so much whether the slogan is right or wrong—no one can deny that Paul, on occasion, does emphasize the cross of Christ. The problem is rather one of perspective and interpretation. (1) How central is this idea in Paul's total view? (2) Even more crucial is the simple question: What is meant by such a theology? Since my own position on these matters is perhaps somewhat unorthodox by comparison with much scholarship, it seems necessary at the beginning to enter into rather detailed discussion of the basic facts upon which interpretation must be based.

The Frequency and the Location of the Motif

Statistics about frequency are the first information needed. The noun "cross" (*stauros*) occurs seven times in the writings I have considered authentic for the purposes of this book. The verb "to crucify" (*stauroō*) appears eight times, and the related term "to crucify with" (*sustauroō*) twice. The total number of occurrences is seventeen. With one possible exception, these are all theological in character; that is, they do more than just point to the historical event of the death of Jesus.

To gain some perspective this statistic may be compared with the frequency of other key terms in Paul's theological vocabulary. The aggregate of the various words from the *dikaioō* root (to justify, justification, righteousness) comes to about one hundred. Theological uses of the word *eirēnē* (peace) amount to about eighteen (apart from the standard appearance of that word in the salutations of his letters). The use of *huios* (son) to denote Jesus Christ and believers as sons occurs about twenty-five times. From a purely statistical count the motif of the cross is not one that Paul mentions very often. Frequency, of course, is not the only or even the basic criterion of the importance of a motif.

What is of more significance in determining the value of a motif to a thinker is to investigate the configurations in his or her writings of the idea. Since, as we have seen, Paul never writes theology in the abstract, but uses his theology to support his practical judgments, the question can be phrased as follows: how often does Paul use the motif of the cross in an important way for his purposes?

The answer is clear and instructive. Paul twice finds the emphasis upon the cross important: once in a section of 1 Corinthians (six occurrences) and, second, throughout the brief Letter to the Galatians (seven occurrences). The remaining four appearances of the motif are scattered throughout several of the other letters: once in Romans (to "crucify with" in 6:6), once in 2 Corinthians, and twice in Philippians. The words are absent in 1 Thessalonians and Philemon. The virtual silence in Romans is important. Not only is it Paul's major theological statement, but it also deals with some of the same issues as does Galatians, where the motif is consistently present. This shows that Paul could easily deal with his major theological conceptions without appeal to a theology of the cross. Of course it may also be possible that he felt it politically inexpedient to use the motif in a letter to the center of the empire.

The motif thus emerges in only two places in concentrated, intentional fashion. This makes it extremely problematic, it seems to me, to claim it as the theological center of Paul's gospel. At times the motif of the cross is important to Paul and he can choose to use it as a major weapon in his arguments. The question now becomes: How does Paul use the motif? That is, how does the concept function in his dealings with his congregations?

There is one important consideration. A motif is not to be rigidly identified with only one set of terms. If function determines language, it may well be that Paul at times uses other terminology, other words, to communicate that motif, as yet undefined, which we are calling the motif of the cross. Thus our study must proceed in two steps. First, the meaning and function of the language of the cross has to be clarified. Second, search for other terminology which might exhibit the same function must be carried out. Only then can we accurately assess the importance and full meaning of the motif (which we have now separated from any single set of terms).

Galatians

Traditionally discussion about Paul's understanding of the cross centers on 1 Corinthians 1—2. It is in Galatians, however, that the central meaning and function emerges most sharply.

While there are uncertainties in our understanding of the situation disclosed by Paul's Letter to the Galatians, the salient issue is clear. Paul established the church on the foundation of a relation to God through Christ independent of Torah obedience. Since the Galatians were Gentiles, this meant that circumcision was unnecessary as entry into the community of God's faithful. At some point before the letter was written, missionaries entered the churches, claiming that circumcision and probably Torah obedience is indeed necessary if the Galatians are to be faithful to God. Paul's description of the gospel is inadequate![1]

The apostle responds passionately in his letter. In every way he can he hammers home his foundational belief: in Christ the way of relating to God through obedience to the laws of Torah has come to an end, being replaced by "faith." This is true for Jews (2:15–16) and thus is certainly true for Gentiles. By and large his arguments remain in the realm of the historical (arguments from the stories in the Torah itself; arguments from human analogies; appeals to the history of the formation of the church).

Once, however, he steps outside the realm of the historical and enters the "mythical" in a very revealing statement.

> Formerly, when you did not know God, you were in bondage to beings that by nature are no gods; but now that you have come to know God, or rather to be known by God, how can you turn back again to the weak and beggarly elements, whose slaves you want to be once more? (Gal. 4:8–9, au. trans.)

One of the basic premises of Paul's whole thought is that the entire human world has been, up until the Christ-event, dominated and controlled by forces and powers hostile to the God who created the cosmos. Paul shares this general world view with apocalyptically oriented Jews as well as believers in Christ. The view is, in fact, pervasive throughout the New Testament.[2] In this passage, when Paul refers to the "weak and beggarly elements," he is speaking of these demonic powers and principalities. Two actual stages and one potential stage of Galatian relationship to these powers are highlighted. *Stage one:* "Formerly," before these Gentiles became believers in Christ, they "served as slaves" "gods that are not by nature gods" (a phrase of delicious irony by Paul). *Stage two:* Now as believers they have been freed by their belief in Christ (freedom is a, or the, major motif in the epistle). They are not now in bondage to such powers. *Potential stage three:* If they accept the Torah as a system of salvation, they return to slavery under these powers. To live under the Torah is "to be enslaved."

Paul thus presents the Galatians with a sharp either-or. There are only two worlds, one under God and the other under the demonic powers. To believe that Torah obedience will bring salvation is to fall into that false world and be enslaved to false gods, "beings that by nature are no gods";

it is the same false world and the same false gods in and under which they had lived as pagans. Only those who have come to know the God revealed in Christ live in the true world under the true God. Thus behind all the historical arguments he marshals lies his premise of the true and the false worlds.

It is in the service of this underlying perspective that his theology of the cross is placed. That is, the motif of the cross functions as the revelation of the true God and thus the true world. The cross of Christ illuminates the character of the true God as self-giving; God disregards and thus rejects the proud and pompous standards of the false world, using as a sign an event considered despicable and dehumanizing by that world. The cross reveals a God who cancels the value placed on achievement and proud performance by human society. For Paul, attempts to secure salvation by Torah obedience are as evidential of living in the false world as are demonstrations by pagans who consciously bow to such "weak and beggarly elements."

This meaning of the cross symbolism is forcefully summed up in the concluding passage in Galatians, where the context makes clear that Paul is still thinking about opposing worlds.

> For even those who receive circumcision do not themselves keep the law, but they desire to have you circumcised that they may glory in your flesh. But far be it from me to glory except in the cross of our Lord Jesus Christ, by which the world has been crucified to me, and I to the world. For neither circumcision counts for anything, nor uncircumcision, but a new creation. (Gal. 6:13–15)

Here "flesh" has the signification it does generally in the rest of the epistle—life "according to the flesh" in its specific manifestation as life lived under justification by works of the law. "Flesh" thus stands for the false world of pride and performance. The cross of Christ is then the vehicle "by which" a person can perceive the falsehood of that world and the truth of that new vision of world. To be crucified to the world means the rejection of and separation from that false world and the freedom to live in the "new creation."

A famous passage with a similar meaning is found in Gal. 2:19–20:

> For I through the law died to the law, that I might live to God. I have been crucified with Christ; it is no longer I who live, but Christ who lives in me; and the life I now live in the flesh I live by faith in the Son of God, who loved me and gave himself for me.

Again the context is the conflict of worlds: *To be crucified with Christ marks the transition between worlds.* It is the same thing as dying to the world—that is, being separated from the world. In Gal. 6:15 the result is a "new creation"; here it is living "by faith in the Son of God," but the parallelism of the two passages suggests Paul means the same thing by the different expressions. Probably it is also fair to suggest a parallelism with the cross of Christ in 6:14 and the phrase here, "The Son of God, who loved me and gave himself for me." If so, then the cross of Christ carries the meaning of the Son's loving and self-giving. And, of course, since it is God who has acted in the Son, this phrase points to the very reality of God "who did not spare his own Son but gave him up for us all" (Rom. 8:32).

The other occurrences of the words denoting crucifixion in Galatians (Gal. 3:1; 5:11, 25; 6:12) are consonant with the meaning in the two passages discussed above. There is, however, one passage in the letter we need to look at, even though those words do not explicitly appear in it. This passage is important for our purpose because Paul here attempts, by a very convoluted and typically rabbinic exegesis, to tie together the death of Jesus with the end of the law.

> For all who rely on works of the law are under a curse; for it is written, "Cursed be every one who does not abide by all things written in the book of the law, and do them." Now it is evident that no man is justified before God by the law; for "He who through faith is righteous shall live"; but the law does not rest on faith, for "He who does them shall live by them." Christ redeemed us from the curse of the law, having become a curse for us—for it is written, "Cursed be every one who hangs on a tree'—that in Christ Jesus the blessing of Abraham might come upon the Gentiles, that we might receive the promise of the Spirit through faith. (Gal. 3:10–14)

The basic claim is clear to any reader, even without any knowledge of hermeneutical niceties: "Christ redeemed us from the curse of the law." The Christ-event means the end of the law as an attempt to earn salvation.

Paul, however, feels compelled to point to the death of Jesus as the particular moment of the Christ-event to be associated with the annulment of the law. He finds in Deut. 21:23 a statement which says that a person executed and subsequently hung on a tree is cursed by God. In another text in Deuteronomy (27:26) he reads that persons who are not faithful in adherence to the law are cursed. He "reads-in" Jesus' death on the cross (the tree) into the first text and into the second he sees a general curse upon all who attempt to subject themselves to Torah obedience.

Since in rabbinic exegesis the meanings of different verses can be transferred one to the other as long as there is at least one word that is common to both texts, Paul now transfers the curse on all Torah followers to the curse on Jesus and can conclude that Christ became a curse for—that is in place of—all actual or would-be Torah followers.[3] In this way he can say that Christ has redeemed us from the law through his death.

Thus even though a word denoting crucifixion does not appear, *Paul explicitly*—and with great intentionality, because with great labor—*relates the cross to the end of the law*. He can then point to the new world as belonging to those who receive the blessing of Abraham and the gift of the Spirit (v. 14). But why does he go to such trouble to make the connection between death (cross) and the end of Torah as a system of salvation? It must be because of what we have deduced from the other texts. As revelation of a God who loves the world and gives in this radical way, the cross is that power of Truth which not only visions the new world but emboldens one to enter it. One participates in the cross insofar as she dares to separate from the old reality ("crucified to the world") and to commit herself ("to live by faith") to the new creation.

1 Corinthians

The theology of the cross also appears in concentrated form in a small but important section of 1 Corinthians (1:10—2:5). Five of the six occurrences of the relevant words in the epistle are located here, the sixth coming in the next and related section (2:8). The words for crucifixion are absent from the rest of the letter.

Thus it is obvious that Paul has a point to make in this section that he thinks can be made most effectively if he pulls this motif out of his barrel of theological ideas. I think it can be said that the basic problem he addresses is the same as in Galatians, but the form in which the problem emerges is completely different. While in Galatians the behavior characteristic of the false world is the pride of performance of the Torah, in the Corinthian community it is the pride of wisdom, of knowledge, of being in possession of "the truth." It is the self-assurance of "knowing what it's all about."[4]

Against this pride of knowing, Paul uses the cross motif, to deflate the pride and to propose a radical alternative, an alternative rooted in the new world where real wisdom and real power are exhibited. Ironically he uses his rhetorical skill to put down the rhetorician. He contrasts "eloquent wisdom" with the power of the word of the cross. The proclamation of the cross is "folly"—folly, that is, to the false world. The inhabitant of the true world, to the contrary, knows that the cross is "the wisdom of God" and the presumed wisdom of the world is folly. Paul plays extensively with this paradox and draws his conclusion: "For the foolishness of God is wiser than humans and the weakness of God is stronger than humans" (1 Cor. 1:25, au. trans.).

The contrast being drawn is clear. It is not between the real wisdom of human society and the actual folly of God. Rather it is between the presumed (but actually false) wisdom of human society and the true wisdom of God, true however much it may seem ridiculous to humanity.

Thus Paul here, as in Galatians, uses his theology of the cross to contrast sharply the true and the false realities of opposing worlds. His aim is to open the door for a perception of that alternative world in which the true God gives herself caringly and thus provides the basis of true perception of reality, that is, the basis of true wisdom. Hence Paul can contrast the boasting of those who claim to know it all with the alternative self-understanding of those who know their life is gift. "He [God] is the source of your life in Christ Jesus, whom God made our wisdom, our righteousness and sanctification and redemption" (1:30). There is only one legitimate boast, and that is to boast in God. Here Paul speaks ironically. To boast in God is really to give up boasting entirely as it is known in the false world.

The Meaning of the Cross

Paul had known a God who as Father prescribed righteous behavior as the criterion for entrance into a proper relationship. While this Father was known to be loving, for Paul at least, this aspect receded behind the image of the demanding father who threatened to kill if the appropriate behavior was not performed. As a result Paul and his Pharisaic colleagues created a world based on the performance principle, in which a person's self-worth—that is his very selfhood—was defined by the doing of the Torah. Paul conformed himself so completely to this image that he performed more than adequately and became a very paragon of such a self (Gal. 1:14; Phil. 3:6).

In God's act in Christ, clearly revealed in the self-giving and radical love of the cross, Paul is forced to acknowledge that the God he had known was not the God who gave so selflessly through his Son. The cross shows what God had always been. The cross also revealed to Paul what true power is. As a result Paul now knows himself differently, not as a person defined by performance but as a self gifted completely by love, as a person secured independently of performance in the divine relationship. Such a new person participates in the cross, because he or she participates in that new world, re-created according to the image of the God "who did not spare his own Son but gave him up for us all" (Rom. 8:32).

If the above is a faithful interpretation of Paul's "theology of the cross," then some meanings frequently attached to the motif both by defenders and detractors of Paul must be rejected.

1. The cross is not a theology of weakness. It is a redefinition of power.

What is normally understood as power—the ability aggressively to dominate and obtain one's will over others—Paul now perceives as weakness. True power is now seen as the freedom to give oneself, the power not to have to dominate.

2. The cross is not a symbol of masochism. This is the case even though throughout the centuries believers have mistakenly chosen masochism as the meaning of Christian "meekness." Thus it is not an exaltation of suffering. To believe in the cross means to live out of true power. Just as God did not give up on her creation, so believers are called to persevering action. It is obvious that Paul knew living in the crucifixion could mean confrontation and battle. It can also involve suffering if and when one's commitment to self-giving brings it as a result. Suffering is thus result, not goal.

3. The cross is not resentment. So Friedrich Nietzsche would have it.[5] For this insightful critic of Christianity, Paul made weakness into a virtue. What Paul could not have, he said one should not have. Those who had true strength Paul resented and projected them into the enemies of God. The gospel of Paul is thus the triumph of weakness and rancor. What Nietzsche failed to see is that Paul knew and exercised the power of domination in his former life. Once the apostle came to experience another kind of power, he was freed from resentment. He could allow others to be different from him, whereas before difference frightened him, hence his attempt in the persecution of followers of Jesus to make others like him.[6]

Related Motifs

We must now look at motifs which frequently have been related to the theology of the cross.

Suffering. It is striking that Paul never says Jesus Christ suffered, or suffers. Were it not for the fact that Paul does write of the "sufferings of Christ" (2 Cor. 1:5; Phil. 3:10), this silence would not be of note. When the apostle refers to the earthly end of Jesus he says that Christ died (1 Cor. 15:3) and that he was obedient (Rom. 5:19). What, then, are the sufferings of Christ? Commentators usually assume the phrase does refer to the death of Jesus. Since, however, these sufferings are not mentioned in the past tense and always in relation to present sufferings of believers, I do not think it completely certain that the phrase refers only to the past.

We may leave that uncertainty aside for the moment and begin with what is clear: The "sufferings of Christ" are never mentioned independently, as if it were a topos in and of itself, but only in relation to the sufferings of Paul and other believers. A complete statement can be found at the beginning of 2 Corinthians.

For as the sufferings of Christ abound in us, so through Christ our comfort abounds as well. . . . And our hope for you has foundation, knowing that as you are sharers in the sufferings, so you are also of the comfort. (2 Cor. 1:5, 7, au. trans.)

The context shows that Paul is referring, with regard to himself, to serious afflictions he has been experiencing. He calls these afflictions "the sufferings of Christ," suggesting some sort of correlation or even identification between what is happening to him and what has happened (or is happening?) to Christ. The Corinthians he confidently (?) asserts are sharers (*koinonoi*) in those sufferings.

Paul makes a similar affirmation about himself in Phil. 3:10–11. On the basis of justification by faith, Paul can now "know him [Christ], both the power of his resurrection and the participation in his sufferings, being conformed to his death, so that I may obtain the resurrection from the dead" (au. trans.).

What is being said here and in other similar, if less explicit passages? Paul and other believers are having difficulties, perhaps physical, perhaps emotional, associated with the gospel. This is the given. The question is how these experiences are to be interpreted and integrated into the larger belief system. The implied affirmation is crucial: *In Paul's view, the new world in which the believer now lives brings suffering because it forces one into conflict with the old world in whatever form, political or religious.* Suffering is not part of the new world in and of itself; remaining true to that new reality may indeed bring suffering. If that happens, suffering is to be accepted as part of the experience of being in the "new creation." The evidence does not suggest that suffering is masochistically lifted up as an essential part of the new world.

Correlation is then made with the sufferings of Jesus Christ. If the correlation is with the sufferings of the earthly Jesus in his death, then it is probably based on the understanding that in his death Jesus was also in conflict with the old world (cf. 1 Cor. 2:8).[7]

On the other hand, it is possible that the sufferings of Christ refer to the present conflict of the resurrected Christ with the old world, a conflict Paul certainly thinks is happening (e.g., 1 Cor. 15:24–28). The conflict which believers have on earth with the old world is a participation in that larger, cosmic battle in which Christ is engaged (see Eph. 6:10–12). Believers are not alone when they suffer as a result of that conflict. Christ is with them and indeed their suffering can be said to be the present sufferings of Christ himself.

Weakness. The theme of weakness, which we have already seen Paul can relate to the cross in 1 Corinthians 1, surfaces also in relation to the quality of life lived by the believer. Just as the cross seems an act of weakness to the old world, so do believers in their lives appear weak to outsiders, even outsiders who presume to be insiders! In the Corinthian correspondence, and especially in 2 Corinthians 10—13, Paul plays on this theme because it is a weapon he thinks useful in his defense-attack against what he considers a false faith based on a "this-worldly" understanding of power.[8]

In this passage the apostle brings all the rhetorical, as well as theological, tricks he can to the argument, including his finely tuned sense of paradox. Weakness is power, and power is weakness. Building on his reference to the "thorn in the flesh," he writes:

> But he said to me, "My grace is sufficient for you, for my power is made perfect in weakness." I will all the more gladly boast of my weaknesses, that the power of Christ may rest upon me. For the sake of Christ, then, I am content with weaknesses, insults, hardships, persecutions, and calamities; for when I am weak, then I am strong. (2 Cor. 12:9-10)

For when I am weak, then I am strong! What can he mean by this logical self-contradiction? In view of the structure of his thought that we have been developing, he cannot be affirming that the believer lives in real weakness, since he has already said that the "weakness of God is stronger than humans" (1 Cor. 1:25). He has to mean here what he meant there, that living in the true world is to live in true strength, to make possible real power, however much it may seem weakness to those living in the false world. True strength comes from accepting life as gift and thus being free to expend oneself in the service of others. It is his way of expressing the paradox stated in the gospels, to lose oneself is to find oneself. Real power belongs to the Mother Teresas of the world!

Suffering and weakness, then, are signs of living on this side of the cross, are marks of being crucified to this world, its values and standards. They are signs, not because the new creation is defined by such realities, but because they reflect the inevitable conflict between the two worlds.

The cross of Christ is, for Paul, a symbol of this new world. By it he points to the radical reversal of reality made possible by God's act in Christ. The cross reveals a God who overflows in gift, who unsparingly graces all people. To live in that new creation frees one to give unsparingly as well and to live in that strength which is not afraid to be called weak by those who do not understand wherein true power lies.

CHAPTER FOUR

THE VICTORY OF GOD
IN CHRIST

Since Paul's understanding of Jesus Christ is centered on *the act of God,* and since, as we have seen, this act is the creation—or recreation—of a new world, Christology necessarily involves a description of the *effect of that act,* both in the present and in the future. If God's act in Jesus Christ has no effect, does not result in the realization of God's intent, then Christology is a futile, academic affair.

Debates on Paul's Understanding

To take this next step throws us into three traditional debates about how best to speak of the effect. These discussions have shown the profound and fruitful tension (or "dialectic") in Paul's theology. We need to be aware of them at the outset.

Christology versus Anthropology

This heading needs definition. The issue is about perspectival priorities. It can be translated into a question: Do believers interpret their selfhood because of what they think Christ has accomplished (the priority of Christology), or do they rather interpret what Christ has accomplished because of the transformation they see effected in themselves (the priority of anthropology)? The debate between two giants of New Testament scholarship, Rudolph Bultmann and Ernst Käsemann, has made this tension acute.[1] Yet the two perspectives have a long history in Christian theology and the issues are immensely complicated.

I am convinced that we need to maintain both perspectives when interpreting Paul. To understand ourselves solely out of an objective description of what God has done in Christ is to court the danger of an intellectualizing and impersonal theology that says nothing to us in the here and now. On the other hand, to "read" our Christology solely out of a presumed change in ourselves is to run toward the opposite danger of imperializing and absolutizing our all-too-partial self-understanding. To eliminate anthropology from consideration gives too little place for the human person. To refuse christological statements that go beyond what we know in ourselves puts the human person too much on center stage.

Individual versus World

Does God's act in Jesus Christ primarily focus upon re-creation of individuals or of all human society? In this traditional debate the church is always a middle term. Is the church a collection of restored individuals or is it that part of the cosmos which reflects God's victory? While the individualistic interpretation has perhaps been the most popular, the corporate, cosmic element in Paul's thinking cannot be ignored. It has again been Käsemann who has argued strongly that God's act is concerned with world, as Paul sees it, and that the individual is best perceived as part of that world.[2] The church is then that community which acknowledges and points to God's victory over world.

The issues and implications are significant, not the least for one's ethical perspective. With the stress placed in previous chapters on re-creation of worlds and world-switching, it should be obvious that I agree with Käsemann that for Paul God's purpose in Christ is directed toward the cosmos. At the same time the apostle certainly does not diminish the significance of the transformed individual. What the cosmic horizon actually does, I believe, is to give the individual a greater dignity and responsibility.

Present versus Future

Does God's act in Jesus Christ focus primarily upon present transformation or does it look to the final eschatological curtain to effect the realization of God's purposes? Here it is widely accepted that Paul affirms both perspectives. "Now but not yet" is a popular slogan among Pauline interpreters, and rightly so. Paul takes both present transformation and future expectation for God's ultimate victory seriously, and any adequate interpretation of Paul's Christology must allow both their due. To deny the present is to vacate it of its immense possibilities for transformation; to deny the future is to retreat into a pessimism which belies Paul's confidence in the ultimate power of God.

These three tensions are interrelated and can be grouped together under the broader headings "objective" and "subjective." Here too the tension must be maintained. To place all the stress upon Christology, world, and future (objective) denies to the present believer any expectation of present fulfillment. To place all stress upon anthropology, individual, and present (subjective) eliminates the ultimate hope for a victory of God which will overcome all opposition to her will.

God's Victory in the
Present

God's intent has always been to create a human community in loving relationship to him. That intent was manifested in the primal creation. In the freedom God gave to humanity humans turned away from that relationship and created a false world based on a false god. That god was perceived as demanding righteous behavior with the ominous threat to kill if obedience was not performed. The false world which thus ensued was a world in which performance and power were the ideals.

God did not give up on the human community and "sent his son" to condemn that false world and to reveal once again the true God, thus to offer humanity the possibility of being restored to a true world in which a true relationship was once again possible. This act of God in Christ attacked the very depths of human consciousness, dove beneath the facade of false self-understanding, and freed persons for a totally new vision of the reality of God. God's act disclosed once again the true God who in Christ justified by grace and who contradicted the standards of the false world by the symbol of the cross. God the Father is no longer the father who threatens to kill but the Father who caringly nurtures the self into a new freedom to accept love.

Victory in Faith

The person who is thus liberated is thrown into a new world. "The old has passed away, behold, the new has come" (2 Cor. 5:17). Since a person *is* the world in which he lives, a new human is created, and it is no casual figure Paul uses when he implies that such a transformation into a new creation is an act of *creatio ex nihilo* by God (1 Cor. 1:28).

This new person lives by and in faith. In fact "faith" is the word Paul uses to describe the quality of life in the new creation. Faith is the new primal perspective by which a person views God and world. It is the life-response to the God who contradicts the false world in the cross. Thus "faith" is the anthropological correlate to the christological "justification by grace." In an earlier book I described faith as "the constant confidence that God has given us our life as sheer gift. It is the courage to remain standing in that place, not to be scared by anxiety, fear, or lack of trust into returning to that old creation based on justification by works."[3]

This new self is gifted with a new mind which, because it perceives true reality, is able to learn God's will (Rom. 12:1–2).[4] Thus not only does this person have a *new being,* he or she is freed for a *new doing* as well. The new person is now able to hear the call of the neighbor and thus to respond in love to that call. New being *and* new doing are described by Paul in terms of freedom, joy, peace, and love.[5]

Victory in Hope

Paul is not so naive as to think that persons always live in the joy and exuberance of faith. While Paul often writes as if he himself had no problems about living in "constant confidence," he can betray at times the opposite (cf. e.g., 2 Cor. 2:12-13). And he certainly is aware that members of his congregations are not always perfect. Even those "thrown" into the new world experience anxiety, doubt, and failure of trust.

Does this mean that a believer in such a situation has again switched worlds, has fallen back into the false world? Not necessarily, because the believer can now stubbornly cling to the knowledge that the true God exists, that the true world is a reality, even if she at the moment does not experience it. Yes, faith is experiential, but it is not to be limited to experience alone. One remains committed to that world. Paul's term for this commitment is "hope."

In this sense hope is as much an experience as is faith. How can we best define hope? Hope is the stubborn conviction in the absence of the experience of fullness that there is indeed a restored world brought into reality by God's act in Christ. If one is careful not to exaggerate, it would be possible to say that hope is an experience of the absence of fullness. This is so because one who can experience an absence knows the opposite to that absence, has in a real way experienced the fullness taken away in the absence, and thus knows that there is something defective in that absence. Paul points in this direction when he says, "If what we do not see [i.e., experience] we hope for, then with patience we eagerly expect it" (Rom. 8:25, au. trans.).

It is indeed in the Letter to the Romans that Paul most consistently develops the theme of hope. Shortly before writing this letter, the apostle had to deal with overly enthusiastic believers in Corinth. They had apparently taken his proclamation of the presence of the new creation to such an extreme that awareness of the equally present old world was either played down or denied (cf. 1 Cor. 1—4). Now conscious of some of the dangers in his own expressions of Christian reality, he writes more cautiously, being careful to point to the "not yet" dimension of the new creation, and, as a consequence, expresses present existence more in terms of hope.[6]

In a rhetorical device known as a "chain" (*catena*) Paul introduces the theme at the very beginning of the major section, Romans 5—8. Suffering leads to endurance, to tested character, to hope, which is "validated" by the presence of the Spirit (5:3–5). Towards the end of this section he returns to the motif, now to develop it in some detail. Present suffering is compared with future glory (8:18). The present is a time of eager expectancy for what is promised in the future, an anticipation which is shared by the whole cosmos (8:19–23). "For in this hope we were saved" (8:24).

The anticipation of the future is indeed so stressed here that the presence of the new creation seems virtually forgotten. Believers do not even know how to pray properly, the apostle laments, and need the assistance of the Spirit itself (8:26). In the final cry of exultation Paul rejoices not in the present power of the kingdom but in the fact that God's love has the power to overcome any obstacle to its relationship with believers. Nothing "will be able to separate us from the love of God in Christ Jesus our Lord" (8:39).

Experience of the presence of the new creation may be lacking. But the apostle knows that the true reality of God is revealed in the Christ-event and that the believer can remain unshakable in that conviction. To know the love of God is to remain placed in that new world, to be able to hope regardless of any obstacle and all anxieties and doubts. Thus whether present experience is one of faith or hope, the source of that new situation is God's act in Jesus Christ.

The Spirit and God's Act
in Christ

Once the subject of a transformed life in the present is raised, however, an apparent problem emerges. There seems to be an overlap in Paul's thinking at this point, because he can just as easily point to the presence of God's Spirit as the source and foundation of the believer's life as he can the event of Jesus Christ. (This problem may seem to be a digression from our topic, but it will lead us into a further dimension of Paul's Christology by forcing the issue of the relation between Jesus Christ and the Spirit of God.)

Early believers apparently experienced powerful surges of power which enabled them to act beyond their normal capacity. They identified the source of this power as the presence of God's Spirit and seem to have associated this presence with the advent of the kingdom of God. In the Corinthian community there were a number of these "manifestations of the Spirit," each of which temporarily distinguished the actor from the normal flow of human activities.

Paul does not deny that these are, indeed, manifestations of the Spirit. His distinctive contribution to the development of the understanding of the Spirit, however, lies in his expansion of its activity to include *all* of the dimensions of the transformed person. Not just occasional and supernatural activities but the total, everyday, and ethical life of the person is a gift of the Spirit. A clear example of this expansion is the catalogue of virtues in Gal. 5:22-23, which Paul claims to be the "fruit of the Spirit."

> But the fruit of the Spirit is love, joy, peace, patience, kindness, goodness, faithfulness, gentleness, self-control; against such there is no law.[7]

But if this is so, then Paul can ascribe the source of the transformed life to the Spirit just as he can to the Christ-event. Was he aware of this seeming overlap and, if so, how did he understand it? His language is certainly fluid. He can introduce the chain already referred to with a reference to the present justification of faith (Rom. 5:1) and conclude it with a reference to God's love which "has been poured into our hearts through the Holy Spirit which has been given to us" (5:5). The Spirit is also said to be the source of eternal life, according to Rom. 8:11, while in Phil. 3:21 it is the act of the resurrected Christ.

Paul reserves the specific terminology of "indwelling" for the activity of the Spirit; yet he can say that Christ is "in" the believer. Romans 8:9-11 clearly shows this fluidity:

> But you are not in the flesh, you are in the Spirit, if in fact the Spirit of God dwells in you. Any one who does not have the Spirit of Christ does not belong to him. But if Christ is in you, although your bodies are dead because of sin, your spirits are alive because of righteousness. If the Spirit of him who raised Jesus from the dead dwells in you, he who raised Christ Jesus from the dead will give life to your mortal bodies also through his Spirit which dwells in you.

Here one can hardly separate conceptually the work of God, Christ, and Spirit. This should suggest that Paul made no real distinctions either. Thus the result of God's act in Christ is manifested in the life of the believer whatever the divine agent named.

We can appreciate the advance Paul made in the conceptualization of the activity of the Spirit within believers. We can also, it seems to me, be understanding of the fluidity, the lack of precision in his thought about the relation of Christ to Spirit—between Christology and pneumatology. (As we will see, the author of the Gospel of John has a greater clarity about the issue and makes a decisive contribution toward a permanent solution.)

There is one passage which may actually show Paul moving toward a more self-conscious identification of Christ and Spirit, although the issues of its interpretation are not easily solved. I can only indicate the statements involved and suggest their possible implication.[8] In 2 Cor. 3:4 Paul begins a long (it extends through 4:6) and somewhat complex comparison between the old and the new covenants or dispensations. A number of contrasts are exhibited, such as that between Moses and Christ and between the kinds of knowledge or truth communicated by these figures. The over-arching contrast, however, is between the old covenant bestowed through Moses and the new covenant "of the Spirit." Paul is "playing with" Exod. 34:29–35, in a way shocking to modern people who expect him to be faith-ful to the literal meaning of the text, but in a way completely acceptable to Jewish exegesis of his day.

Since both Christ and Spirit are agents of the new covenant, it is not sur-prising that here Paul writes of their interrelationship. He can say in 2 Cor. 3:17 that "the Lord is the Spirit," yet write immediately after in the same verse of "the Spirit of the Lord." In 3:18 he clearly wants to state that a relation exists but his Greek remains ambiguous about *what* the relation-ship is. No certainty is possible.

We cannot go into the disputed exegesis.[9] I simply want to suggest that in 2 Cor. 3:4—4:6 ambiguity is rampant. God, Christ, and Spirit all func-tion at one time or another as actors. Had Paul been clear in his mind about how Christ and Spirit explicitly related to each other, he surely would have written with greater clarity.

Thus even in this passage we have to draw the conclusion taken above, that the apostle somewhat unselfconsciously identifies the work of God through Christ and through Spirit. He is, after all, at the very beginning of the development of thinking about extremely difficult issues, thinking which will ultimately culminate in the doctrine of the Trinity in later cen-turies.

God's Victory in the Future

Paul is not a pessimist. Buffeted about, harrassed, threatened with death, faced with the refusal of his own people to accept the work of God in Christ, he nevertheless staunchly looks to the future for the ultimate victory of God's act in Jesus Christ.[10] We often see Paul's march through the Roman Empire as a successful, conquering parade. Perhaps we do not want to acknowledge how struggling his congregations were and how precari-ously even his "successes" perched, teetering between dangers from within and without. Most scholars today view his communities as small "house churches," a miniscule collection of partly ragtag people seen over against the larger society.

Yes, Paul can celebrate the victory of God in Christ in the lives of believers in the present. His vision, however, is cosmic. Despite the com-parative paucity of present results, he looks to the future for a total victory of God's act in Christ over all of God's creation. More important than Paul's human march through the cities is the divine procession toward that ultimate, cosmic conclusion.

In a hymn the apostle cites in Phil. 2:6–11, the early church expressed its confidence in that ultimate victory which they saw already signaled in Christ's resurrection. In the conclusion of the hymn the resurrection is portrayed as an enthronement ceremony:

Therefore God has highly exalted him
  and bestowed on him the name above all other names;
that in the name of Jesus every knee should bow—
  heavenly, earthly, and subterranean;
and every tongue confess that the Lord is Jesus Christ,
  to the glory of God the Father.
                             (Phil. 2:9–11, au. trans.)

Here all do obeisance to the enthroned Lord Jesus Christ, and most scholars today think that the knees and tongues at least include the cosmic powers and principalities to whom the human race has up to now been subjected.

However the hymn may have been understood in the early communities, Paul himself knows this obeisance is ultimately a future, not a present reality. The powers and principalities still stand in the way of God's ultimate victory, even if they cannot separate the believer from his love (Rom. 8:37–39). Thus the work of Christ continues now and into the future until that ultimate triumph.

Then comes the end, when he [the exalted Christ] delivers the kingdom to God the Father after destroying every rule and every authority and power. For he must reign until he has put all his enemies under his feet. The last enemy to be destroyed is death. (1 Cor. 15:24–26)

Here the work of Christ continues: he is the warrior who as God's vice-regent fights the divine battle against the powers hostile to God's sovereignty.

There are other motifs to which Paul occasionally refers, indicating further that he conceives the work of Christ as continuing in the present and into the future. In the elaborate image of the divine law court in Rom. 8:31–34, not only is God the judge on the side of the believers, but the resurrected Christ is described as being at the right hand interceding for them. Christ functions as the "defense attorney" who defends the believers from any accusations.[11]

The ultimate act of God in Christ is the overcoming of death and the bestowal of a glorious resurrection existence. The warrior Christ will overthrow death as the last enemy (1 Cor. 15:26). The savior Christ will reform our mortal bodies into his heavenly likeness.

But our commonwealth is in heaven, and from it we await a Savior, the Lord

Jesus Christ, who will change our lowly body to be like his glorious body, by the power which enables him even to subject all things to himself. (Phil. 3:20-21)

Paul thus looks forward to the completion of God's act in Christ as an ultimate cosmic victory. Elements of this victory have already been mentioned. The cosmic enemies will be dethroned. Believers will live in the eternal reign of God. In some way the entire creation is incorporated into this victory (Rom. 8:22-23). He anticipates that his people will have a place in this eternal reign: "All Israel will be saved" (Rom. 11:26). Unbelievers apparently have death as their ultimate fate (cf. 2 Cor. 4:3). At any rate he never suggests any belief in eternal torment.

Does this mean that Paul believes in the universal salvation of all people? Is such an expectation the ultimate conclusion to his confidence in the power of God's act in Christ? As we have seen, his various, apparently conflicting, statements on the matter do not give great confidence in knowing his mind.

Again one concludes that Paul had not thought the matter through to a dogmatic conclusion. That he could think of such an amazing victory of God is possible. At least the exultant conclusion to his intense wrestling with his hope for Israel so suggests:

For God has consigned all people to disobedience that he may have mercy upon all. (Rom. 11:32, au. trans.)

CHAPTER FIVE

WHO JESUS CHRIST WAS
AND IS

Up to this point I have concentrated entirely on Paul's description of God's act in Jesus Christ. Since this is Paul's own primary focus, such concentration is appropriate. The kinds of questions so many believers over the ages have asked—Who was Jesus, or who is he? Was he human? Is he divine? How can we understand the confluence of human and divine in Jesus Christ? How does the divinity of Jesus relate to Trinitarian theology?—all these were at best secondary to Paul. His answers to them, were we able to reconstruct them, might appear naive in comparison with the systematic work of later theologians self-conscious of these issues and the problems they brought.

This means that Paul was much more concerned with *the work* of Jesus Christ than he was with *the person* (see chap. 1). Since we today do ask questions about person, however, it is not only legitimate but even necessary to ask them even of a theologian who did not ask them himself.[1] At least we may do so as long as we do not judge a first-century thinker by fourth-century standards. Paul was, we must keep reminding ourselves, at the very beginning of the process.

Someone might object. What difference does it make who Jesus was or is if we can affirm with conviction what God has done in the Christ-event? This seemingly simple question, with its attempt to short-circuit questions about person, founders on the sharp rock of logic. Granted that the assertions about act may have faith priority over those about nature, the one necessitates the other. Who must Jesus be in order for one to be able to make certain statements about what God has done through him? I doubt that Paul himself ever raised that question. It does seem fair, however, to inquire whether Paul, however unreflective, has a basic coherence in his Christology. The author of the Gospel of John, as we will see, is much more self-conscious about the importance of this question.

A great gulf inevitably separates Paul from later christological reflection. It concerns the question about person, specifically reflections about the nature of God's person. Israelite and early Jewish theologians never thought about God in terms of nature. In their thought world, God was conceived in terms of act and will. It is what God does that defines God's reality. The implications for Christology are clear. If Jesus Christ does what God is believed to do, then in that sense Jesus Christ is "divine." In such a conceptuality, in fact, it is perhaps legitimate for questions about person to be dissolved into questions about act. This is, in my judgment, the reason why Paul does not self-consciously reflect upon matters of person which later theologians, working from a different conceptuality, will find crucial.

The Person of Jesus Christ

With the above always in mind, we can turn to Paul's description of the person of Jesus Christ. Who was and is this person in and through whom God's eschatological act occurred?

The Humanity of Jesus

Almost all scholars today think that for Paul the earthly Jesus was completely human. Yet, as far as the evidence goes, the apostle was not very interested in the Jesus "according to the flesh," and he writes rather casually about the earthly Jesus when he does need to say something about him.

This casualness, this unreflectiveness, could imply some ambivalence about the full humanity of Jesus and has occasionally been so taken. Much more likely, however, is that Paul never faced claims that Jesus was not human, as would have been the case had Paul lived a few decades later. It is opposition that makes a person clarify his language. No one could doubt the position of the author of 1 John. "Every spirit which confesses that Jesus Christ has come in the flesh is of God, and every spirit which does not confess Jesus [having come in the flesh] is not of God" (4:2–3). He writes so specifically because, obviously, some people have been denying Jesus' humanity. Paul has not faced such claims, and this adequately explains the less-than-specific character of his language.

Perhaps the clearest statement occurs in Galatians. God sent the Son, "Born of woman, born under the law" (Gal. 4:4). Similarly he writes in Romans, in the same "sending the Son" language, that Jesus was sent "in the likeness of sinful flesh and for sin" (Rom. 8:3). The only question here involves the use of the noun "likeness" (*homoiōma*). While uncertainty will remain about the exact nuance of Paul's meaning, modern exegetes seem agreed in believing that it does not mean that Jesus was like, but not really, human. The word can simply be taken to mean "form" in the sense of reality: "In the reality of sinful flesh."[2]

If Jesus is human, he is not thereby the powerful agent pictured in the Gospels. Paul never mentions Jesus as teacher (let alone a powerful, victorious teacher) or Jesus as miracle worker. Thus the almost-more-than-human Jesus of the Gospels, the all-powerful "divine man," has no part in Paul's Christology. The human Jesus is a hidden actor, not the glorious manifestation of divine power.

Is then the humanity of Jesus just assumed by Paul or is it important to his christological affirmations? Only, I think, at one point. When Paul proclaims a Messiah crucified (1 Cor. 2:2), he is using the most tragic moment of Jesus' humanity to exhibit the world-reversal revelation of God's act in Christ. That God's Son *as human being* was crucified makes visible the heart of the radically different world Paul calls people to enter.

The Postresurrection Existence of
Jesus Christ

For Paul, Jesus is raised by God to become a "spiritual body" (1 Cor. 15:44). This does not mean that Jesus now transcends human existence but rather that his humanity has been transformed into that perfect existence which is God's intention for all humankind.[3] The resurrected Jesus is moreover a "life-giving spirit" (1 Cor. 15:45), "who will change our lowly body to be like his glorious body, by the power which enables him even to subject all things to himself" (Phil. 3:21). In his earthly life Jesus manifested the obedience of the faithful person; in his resurrection life he enjoys the perfection of God's intent for persons and the power to transform the believer into that same perfection.[4]

The Present Reign of Jesus Christ

Between the time of Jesus' transformation and that of the believers, Jesus reigns as cosmic lord. The resurrection has significance that far transcends the results to the person of Jesus. He is enthroned (Phil. 2:9–11) and fights on God's behalf for the ultimate restoration of the cosmos to God's will (1 Cor. 15:24–27).[5] As God's vice-regent, the resurrected Christ carries out God's will for the cosmos.

In this sense—that Christ acts out God's will and power—it can be said that for Paul Jesus Christ is divine. But this means that Christ functions as God, not that he is divine by "nature" (which would probably not have meant anything to Paul in the conceptuality in which he lived). Since God is defined as will and act, and since the resurrected Christ acts as God, he manifests God's own act and will.

The Ultimate Subordination of the Son

The impossibility of applying "nature" concepts to Paul's Christology is highlighted by his depiction of the final event in God's act of restoration.

In 1 Cor. 15:28, Paul says explicitly: "When all things are subjected to him [the reigning Christ], then the Son himself will also be subjected to him [i.e., God] who put all things under him, that God may be all in all" (au. trans.). Once the victory is won, the reigning Christ, now no longer needing to function as God, subjects himself to the ultimate power, and God finally stands alone on center stage. Whatever the precise meaning Paul intended by his last clause, "that God may be all in all," it must mean at least this: Once the series of acts culminating in the final victory of God over her world is completed, God remains the only and single power who is God. All other realities, including Jesus Christ, submit as subjects to that ultimate Lord. Paul does not say it, but it seems fair to suggest that this subordination is the final act of the obedience of the Son.

The Preexistence of Jesus Christ

We can now turn back to the initial stage of the reality of Jesus Christ: his preexistence. Affirmations of such preexistence developed early in the church, although the belief was not shared by all (none of the Synoptics, for example, show clear evidence of the idea). The hymn cited by Paul in Philippians 2 and the early liturgical form in Col. 1:15–16 seem to reflect this belief, and it reaches a height in the Gospel of John. Paul is aware of belief in preexistence, yet reference to it emerges in his writings only when he seems to be citing or alluding to formulas created by others in the church.[6]

Nowhere does he develop the motif in his own theological reflections. Preexistence clearly does not have an essential function in his christological structure. We could put it this way—in Paul's conceptualization, God's act of justification and revelation in the cross and resurrection of Jesus can be affirmed without the claim of preexistence.

One could question Paul at this point. Does not his language of "sending"—"God sent his Son"—imply and even demand the idea of preexistence? Does not the identification of the event of Jesus Christ with God's power and will ultimately and logically force the conclusion that the reality of Jesus Christ must exist prior to the incarnation?[7] Would Paul have been content to say, in lieu of the sending language, that "God chose a man, Jesus, in order to . . ."? I am not sure he would have been happy with such an alternative. These are perhaps, however, unfair questions, and we should remain content with what Paul does and does not say.

The Titles

So far I have tried to sketch the basic contour of Paul's understanding of the person of Jesus, both in his earthly and his resurrection existence.

Before we summarize, however, it is necessary to look at the titles Paul uses when he is writing about Jesus. What he calls Jesus is clear. To determine why he uses the titles he does is, however, a surprisingly difficult question to answer. With one exception (the last Adam—which is not really a title) Paul has inherited the titles from the church. He uses them in such non-discriminating fashion that they may add little to his communication about the meaning of Jesus.

First, one should notice what titles he does not employ.

Son of Man. This was perhaps the earliest title used to point to the significance of Jesus in the churches. As we will see, it was still a crucial title in Johannine circles at the time of the Gospel. Paul never uses it. The standard reason given for Paul's refusal to apply it to Jesus is that it would have made little sense to Greeks not accustomed to Jewish apocalyptic terminology. Whether this is an adequate explanation is another matter. (Paul is not always so accommodating to the intellectual horizons of his readers.) Given the popularity of this title in the Gospels, Paul's silence is, in fact, rather surprising, but all we can do here is to point to his decision not to use it.

Apart from the formulaic citation in Rom. 1:3 he never calls Jesus the *Son of David.* Only once (Phil. 3:20) does he use the term *Savior (sotēr)*, a title which will later become popular. He does, however, use the verb to point to the act of God in Christ. For Paul the titles are *Christ (christos)*, *lord (kyrios)*, and *Son of God (hyios tou theou)*, a list to which we must append the notion of *the last Adam.*

Christ. Christos is a translation of the Hebrew *messiaḥ* (literally "anointed"). In the Gospels it does not occur often and seems subordinated to the title Son of man. (It must be kept in mind that the Gospels as written documents all come from a time later than Paul's letters.) In the apostle's vocabulary, however, *christos* occurs frequently (about 275 times) and in every possible context. Paul's usage shows that the title is well on its way to becoming a proper name, a process clearly visible in most of the New Testament writings other than the Gospels.

This compels the conclusion that *christos* quickly became a popular title in Hellenistic Christianity, perhaps because there it could be more easily separated from its political and militaristic roots. However that may be, our task is to ask about Paul's use. How does the term function in Paul's Christology?

On the one hand, it seems to be at times a proper name, in which case it has no specific christological function. On the other hand, it is certainly at times a title of honor, completely denuded from its original political meaning.[8] To say more than this is to enter murky waters. Paul does not have a single meaning which is pointed to by the term. There may, however, be a certain relationship between the term and Paul's reflections on Jesus' death.[9] *Christos* can occur without other titles in this context.

> Christ died for our sins in accordance with the scriptures. (1 Cor. 15:3)
> We preach Christ crucified. (1 Cor. 1:23)
> At the right time Christ died for the ungodly. (Rom. 5:6)
> Christ redeemed us from the curse of the law. (The context here is the crucifixion of Jesus.) (Gal. 3:13)

It is widely held that 1 Cor. 15:3 is a pre-Pauline formula. To the extent that the relation between title and death is consciously intended, it was not created by Paul himself.

The question becomes what we learn about the significance of Jesus' death due to the association of *christos* with it. In Jewish thought, the Messiah had a royal function. That the Messiah would die, let alone perform a salvatory effect through his death, does not seem to have been part of such thinking during the early decades of the first century.[10] The association would thus have been made by Christians themselves. In part this may have been a dramatic attempt to explain the death of Jesus. In a logic-defying thought, the early believers claimed that his death was not a tragic accident, but part of the very role God's Messiah was to play. In part it may also have been self-conscious irony in opposition to Jewish theology. In contrast to a theology of a glorious, royal Messiah, a suffering, dying Messiah was proclaimed. I do not see that it is possible to move beyond such speculations to surer ground.

Even if the association with death was occasionally in Paul's mind, it does not dominate his use of the title. In 1 Corinthians 15, having used the title in the formulaic reference to Jesus' death, he proceeds to write about the resurrection using *christos* virtually without exception. In Romans 5, after using the title twice with reference to the death, he switches to the use of "Son" two verses later, while continuing to write about his death. We have to conclude that since the title can point to any dimension of God's act in Jesus Christ, it is the context that gives meaning to the title, not the reverse.

Kyrios. This title has in Greek culture a wide range of meanings, from the polite "Sir" to a term implying complete subjection by the speaker to an absolute master. In the latter spectrum *kyrios* can refer to a military leader, a king, a god (with the correlate *kyria* for a goddess), and to the Roman emperor. In Hellenistic Judaism the title was used of Yahweh (e.g., Philo).

Scholars have devoted much energy to discover the backgrounds for early Christian use of the title for Jesus, and it is not necessary to recapitulate that elaborate discussion here.[11] Probably it is safe to conclude that there are multiple "backgrounds" involved. Once believers acclaimed the resurrected Jesus to be the cosmic power, it is scarcely conceivable that they would not have used *kyrios* in their acclamations.

In Paul the term is ever-present, though not with the frequency of *christos*. While, as we saw, *christos* occurs about 275 times, *kyrios* appears approximately 190. Thus we expect that the title should appear in each of his letters somewhat less often than *christos*. This is the case with 2 Corinthians, Philippians, and Romans. In 1 Thessalonians, however, *kyrios* dominates over *christos*, while in 1 Corinthians it appears slightly more frequently than *christos*. In Galatians, on the other hand, "Lord" (5 times) is markedly subordinate to "Christ" (37 occurrences). This suggests that Paul is not completely indiscriminate in his choices, that in some contexts he prefers one over the other.

Whatever the backgrounds of Paul's usages, the fact is that "Lord" is a dynamic title, always in correlation, whether explicit or implicit, with *doulos,* a servant or slave (in Greek the term means both). On the one hand, *kyrios* points to the resurrected Jesus as cosmic ruler (as in the hymn believers sing to Jesus as *kyrios Jesus christos* in Phil. 2:11). It points to the status and function of the enthroned Christ, not to substance or nature.

On the other hand, it implies that the believer is servant or slave of Jesus the Lord. In the beginning of Romans Paul calls himself, even in his exalted status as apostle, the *doulos* of Jesus Christ (1:1). The ministers to the Corinthians are, he says, to be seen as servants (here the Greek is *hyperetai*) of Christ. This relation applies, of course, to all believers, so that "he who was called in the Lord as a slave is a freedman of the Lord. Likewise he who was free when called is a slave of Christ" (1 Cor. 7:22). (Paul is not here saying that slaves to human masters are not also servants of the Lord.)

Yes, God is the gracious Father who gives life to all through Jesus Christ, and Christ is the "first-born among many brethren" (Rom. 8:29). Paul does not want the believers to forget, however, that the resurrected Jesus is also the Lord of their lives, and obedience should be to him (and him alone).

Paul, for example, is not opposed to marriage, yet he is unhappy that it creates divided loyalties.

I want you to be free from anxieties. The unmarried man is anxious about the affairs of the Lord, how to please the Lord; but the married man is anxious about worldly affairs, how to please his wife, and his interests are divided. (1 Cor. 7:32–34)

To call Jesus *kyrios* is thus to acknowledge that obedience to him is primary and that subjection should be single-minded. At the same time it needs to be emphasized that obedience to this *kyrios* means trust in a divine power that graces all with joyful and truly human existence. To be *doulos* to this Lord means to live in the power of the new creation. Martin Luther expressed Paul's paradox cleanly: "A Christian is a perfectly free lord of all, subject to none. A Christian is a perfectly dutiful servant of all, subject to all."

Hyios tou theou. Compared with *christos* and *kyrios* Paul uses "Son" to refer to Jesus only 15 times. This usage represents either a very casual or a very selective interest in the term. Eleven of the 15 occurrences are in Galatians and Romans, while the title does not appear at all in Philippians or Philemon. Given the rarity of Paul's use of the word, disparity among the various letters is not significant.

We must again forego discussion of the possible backgrounds of Paul's usage. There were, of course, many sons and daughters of gods in pagan mythology, while in the Hebrew Bible and early Judaism Israel as well as individual human servants (including kings, and therefore perhaps including the Messiah) were designated as God's son(s). The question for us must again be the functional one: How does Paul use the title "Son" when applied to Jesus Christ?

One thing is clear: the correlate to Jesus as "Son" is not God as Father. In only one instance (1 Cor. 15:28) is Jesus as Son brought into any explicit relationship with God as Father (and here the titles are separated by four verses). This means, conversely, that the 22 times Paul refers to God as Father do not include in the immediate context any correlation with Jesus as Son. The two linguistic metaphors are completely discrete.

In 11 of the 15 instances the phrase "his Son" occurs, while in 3 of the remaining 4 the full title "Son of God" appears. Only once is "the Son" used absolutely. In all of the instances the correlate term for the divine in the immediate context is *theos*, God. Hence the explicit or implied title we have to deal with is Son of God (*hyios tou theou*), not Son of the Father (*hyios tou patrou*).

Once separated from the notion of familial metaphor, can we then specify just how Paul uses "Son of God"? Even with such few occurrences, it is not possible to make an equation between title and a single function. There seem to me two clusters of texts that are important.

First, Paul uses the title "Son" when he wants to correlate God as closely as possible with the act in Christ. God sent "his own Son" to condemn sin (Rom. 8:3). God sent "his Son" to redeem people from the law (Gal. 4:4–5). God did not "spare his own Son, but gave him up for us all" (Rom. 8:32). The death of "his Son" accomplishes reconciliation with God (Rom. 5:10). Nuanced somewhat differently, in Gal. 2:20 Paul writes that the Son of God "loved me and gave himself for me." This cluster suggests that Paul at times wants to emphasize God's total investment in the salvatory process. God is not a distant observer: she is involved in the lowly and self-giving act of her Son.

Second, Paul also uses Son of God when he wants to point to the sonship of believers. In a carefully constructed passage in Galatians Paul ties the past act of the Son and the present act of the "Spirit of the Son" with adoption and sonship. The structure of the passage can be laid out in abbreviated form.

> When the fullness of time came,
> God sent out his Son . . .
>   that we might receive adoption as sons.
> And because you are sons,
> God sent out the spirit of his Son into our hearts crying "abba" (Father).
>   Thus you are no longer a slave but a son; and if a son, also an heir through God.
>
> (Gal. 4:4–7, au. trans.)

The past act of the Son results in the Galatian Gentiles being adopted into the people of God. The present act of "the spirit of his Son" incorporates them into present filiation, signaled by the cry of *abba*.[12]

In Rom. 8:29 God is said to have conformed the existence of believers "to the image of his Son, in order that he might be the first-born among many brethren." Paul also says the Corinthians have been called into the "fellowship of [with?] his Son, Jesus Christ our Lord" (1 Cor. 1:9).

These two clusters of texts affirm what seem to be strikingly opposite ideas. The first makes an intimate relation between God and Jesus Christ. The second makes an equally intimate relationship between Jesus Christ and the believers. The temptation is then to think that the title "Son of God" might be a bridge title, used to unite God with believers through the Son, somewhat like the indwelling thought of the Gospel of John.[13] The texts do not suggest, however, that Paul desired to create such a union, and we will do well to view these clusters as discrete conceptualizations in Paul's Christology.

"Son of God" is thus used by Paul to point to certain acts by God and certain relationships. Since Paul does not conceive of relationships substantively, it is a serious error to take his use of "son" as support for later credal discussions about *homoousia* (i.e., Father and Son are of the same substance or nature). Oscar Cullmann is correct: "It is only meaningful to speak of the Son in view of God's revelatory action, not in view of his being."[14]

The last Adam. This phrase, which occurs only once in Paul (1 Cor. 15:45), certainly does not qualify as a title. Since, however, it points to a contrast between the first Adam's disobedience and its consequences and the salvatory act of Jesus Christ, a point discussed at some length in Romans 5 and 1 Corinthians 15, the function Paul affixes to the motif needs a brief mention.[15]

The key part of the contrast is the radical difference in the results of the two actors. Adam through sin brought death. Jesus through obedience brings life. Jesus Christ is the eschatological (the real meaning here of "last") act which reverses the fate of humanity caused by Adam. Although the theme of obedience stressed in Romans 5 seems to point to the earthly Jesus as the last Adam, it is really the resurrection of Jesus that opens the way toward the transformation of believers into the reality always promised by God, now effected through Jesus Christ. Thus it is the resurrected Christ who bestows—or will bestow—the transformed existence on believers. This motif is not unrelated to the theme of the sonship of believers and is beautifully expressed in Phil. 3:20–21.

> But our commonwealth is in heaven, and from it we await a Savior, the Lord Jesus Christ, who will change our lowly body to be like his glorious body, by the power which enables him even to subject all things to himself.

Conclusion

Paul is totally absorbed in the excitement of the new world and its possibilities for human existence brought about by God's act in Jesus Christ. With all his intensity he wants to communicate the vision of what God has done: God powerfully revealed through the cross his true reality as the gracious giver of life *and* the corresponding reality of the true creation, a world which lives in self-giving love rather than anxious self-aggrandizement. In this world faithful citizens live in confidence that life is gift, a life of "justification by grace." The false world is hastening to its dreary end, and the victorious power of God in Christ will soon conquer the last vestiges of rebellion. The perfection of that world will be realized in the final resurrection of all people who have shown their willingness to trust in that God Paul sees revealed in Christ.

Paul has learned about this new world through what early believers were already affirming about Jesus Christ—in their words and their community life—and through what he believes is direct encounter with divine power, a power sufficient to free Paul from his stubborn reliance on the false world and its presumed truth and power. Thus, as Paul works out his understanding about this radical change in world, he has a certain set of givens. The man Jesus, crucified by Roman authority, resurrected by the power of God, now sits at the right hand of God and by the power invested in him by God will soon bring into perfect realization that world.

The apostle accepts this basic pattern and most of the titles given Jesus by the church. This pattern has been called a "three-stage" Christology.[16] First, he acknowledges the preexistence of the Christ-event but places little emphasis upon it. Second, he accepts or assumes that Jesus lived a human life but places little weight upon that part as well. Jesus was obedient, but nothing of the powerful teacher and actor portrayed by the Gospels comes through in the Pauline texts. Finally, all importance is attached to the third stage begun by death and resurrection, continuing in present lordship and culminating in ultimate victory.

In this third stage Jesus Christ acts as God's agent in restoring God's world. In this sense the resurrected Christ functions as God. "Lord," "Son," "last Adam," and sometimes "Christ" point to dimensions of this function; they do not point to claims of substantive identity with God. Indeed, in a crucial way the resurrected Christ remains human, transformed into eschatological perfection, and it is through him that faithful believers will be able to participate in that ultimate human perfection themselves.

According to Paul the final act of the exalted Christ is to give up his exalted status and to submit himself to God the ultimate sovereign. God alone remains God, as Paul concludes in his theocentric benediction at the end of his theological revisioning in Romans:

For from him and through him and to him are all things.
To him be glory for ever.

(Rom. 11:36)

PART 2

THE CHRISTOLOGY OF JOHN

CHAPTER SIX

THE THEOLOGICAL SETTING OF
THE GOSPEL OF JOHN

No story of any length is simple or its author single-minded. While a writer may self-consciously intend to make a single point, inevitably secondary issues impinge on her intended purpose. Of some of these the author is aware; others will slip into the narrative undetected and unintended by her. But because this author is complex and the situation she addresses equally complex, the story will emerge with several levels, more than one plot, and inevitably subject to more than one interpretation.

Any one who has studied the Gospel of John in depth knows that its story amply satisfies expectations of complexity.[1] So apparently simple on the surface, so stratified in its many levels of meaning! The reader finds its sentences at times obvious, at times frustratingly opaque. There are spaces of monochromatic brightness, while others are intricately subtle in chiaroscuro. Small wonder that the scholarly world in general considers this book to be the most profound of all the writings in the New Testament.

As a story about Jesus of Nazareth it focuses more centrally on the christological issues than any other New Testament document, more even than the other Gospels. It is, indeed, the christological statement of early Christianity and thus the climactic segment in a study of early interpretations of Jesus Christ.

But while this Gospel may be profound, its complexity defies any single attempt to exhaust its meaning. Even interpreters who have probed most deeply differ among themselves. In part this is no doubt due to our inability to locate the author and his community adequately in time, place, and environment. In part it is because of the levels discovered in the story. R. Alan Culpepper comments fairly: "Like most good plots and all good characters, John and its Jesus retain areas of shadow and mystery it will not illuminate for the reader. That is part of its power and its fascination."[2]

Nevertheless, for our purposes we need a principle of organization, a perspective to help us contend with the basic christological witness made by the Gospel of John. To find this perspective we begin with a question: What is the basic issue or problem the author deals with when he tells the story? If there is one, and if we can discover it, then John's Christology must be his solution to that problem.

Of course the process of our discovery would be the reverse of the logic expressed. It is how the author tells the story that gives us clues to the problem with which he struggles. To seek for the basic issue does not imply that the Gospel deals with only a single issue. All we have said so far suggests the contrary. Nevertheless, if we could discover what lies at the heart of his reflection, then all the other issues could be related to this primary concern, and we would ideally have before us a web of interrelated themes.

I do not mean to suggest that the author is a philosopher who constructs a view of Jesus simply to solve logical or existential problems. Nevertheless, the Gospel of John is to be placed at a late stage in the struggle of the Johannine community for self-understanding. It reflects energetic debates with the Jewish community.[3] In this tension-filled crucible the author has formed a story about Jesus to deal with the issues raised by these struggles. John has told the story in such a way that it profoundly and artistically witnesses to his faith.

The Problem

I want to propose that we can discover the basic issue! The problem, as I see it, is simple: How does one know that truth to which one must commit one's life? John has found his answer in Jesus Christ the Word. Through the narrative of the Gospel he tries to show how, indeed, Jesus is the way to Truth. The question is prior to and more basic than the question about the content, the substance of truth. If I claim such and such to be true, the immediate counter can be, how do I know it is true? What is my authority? What is the status of the authority on which I make my claim?

Like all profound problems, it is as simple as it is logically insoluble. The issue transcends intellectual curiosity; it is a problem that demands address despite the fact that it has no final logical solution. One's life is at stake in this question, since the answer one arrives at forms or transforms one's total existence, for good or ill.

This problem has been debated in all cultures by serious philosophical and religious thinkers. Greek philosophy struggled for solutions and set the tone for discussions in the Hellenistic world, not the least of which were the sometimes baroque but nevertheless intense reflections of the Gnostics.[4] For theologians the solution obviously involved some description of god or gods and how he, she, they, or it related to the sensible world in which humans are placed (or trapped).

In a simple world whose inhabitants assume the truth of their structure, anxiety about relationships with the ultimate does not ordinarily surface in acute fashion. There is a naive consensus, which is likely to be more implicit than stated. Once, however, critical questions do begin to be raised, once competing claims are voiced, then the question is raised to the self-conscious level. The struggle begins in earnest and critical reflection becomes necessary.[5]

It is in such a self-conscious and conflictive world that we must place the Gospel of John. Hellenistic religious thinkers agonized about the appropriate ways of stating the problem and fought with each other about solutions. Even within broadly accepted parameters thinkers had begun to refine and redefine commonly accepted conclusions. The author of the Gospel found himself inside such intense debate.[6]

While within Judaism the Torah was the accepted constitution whose ultimate author was God, how to interpret this constitution had come to be discussed and disputed. The question about interpretation raised the ultimate question about access to the truth. How is Yahweh and his will revealed? Pharisees had their own answers; they argued among themselves about them. So did Sadducees and the emerging mystical and Gnostic traditions. Philo indicates that at least some Hellenistic Jews were struggling with their own answers.[7]

The Jewish sect which would come to be called Christianity complicated the internal problem. With its reliance upon Jesus, however interpreted, a new and unique solution to the problem was implied. In some way believers in Jesus Christ claimed by their very commitment that it was through this one person that God was most truly known and her will made visible for the human community. Sooner or later, the implicit tension between Jesus and Torah had to become explicit. The author of the Gospel of Matthew is sensitive to the problem and tries to hold these two "sources" together in creative tension. The author of John was, however, more keenly aware of this issue than any other early Christian thinker. The very situation of conflict with neighboring Jews, so visible in chapters 5—12 of the Gospel, made such awareness impossible for him to repress.

Both Judaism and emerging Christianity offered competing claims. Even within the church various ways of working out the implications of the centrality of Jesus had emerged. Through his story of Jesus, John makes a distinctive contribution to understanding how this truth is to be comprehended, one often at variance with other suggestions. Thus our author not only must attend to Jewish disagreement with Christian claims, but also must show that his own radical interpretation of Christianity is justified. It is to John's credit that he sees that his position stands or falls with the integration of *who* Jesus is with *how* this Jesus can reveal ultimately the divine will.

The Approach to a Solution

John's answer unfolds as he tells the story (see the following chapters). Here I will lay out the basic structure within which John works and from which he perceives the correct approach to a solution. It is a radical, either-or structure, comfortable neither to enlightened ancients nor to contemporary liberals today. Before we make judgments upon it, however, we will need to listen carefully to how he uses this structure. First I am going to describe his perspective in terms not his own but which have frequently been used of his views. This seems fair, as long as we keep in mind that we are importing concepts and perhaps nuances of meaning.

For John reality is separated into two realms: the realm of the divine—the *transcendent*—and that of the world—the *immanent*.[8] The transcendent world is where Truth is, that is, ultimate reality. To know, to participate in this realm is thus the ultimate aim of the serious human person. The question is how?

To the world, to immanent reality, belong humans in all the dimensions of their existence—flesh, emotions, and mind.[9] *Thus the products of human thinking belong to the immanent—the world(s) constructed by human communities, including religious systems.* Religion and theology in and of themselves are purely human constructions and belong to the immanent, not the transcendent world.

But if this is so, then how can one know what ultimate reality is and how it impinges upon a person? There is, in John's cosmology, no way the human mind can think through to divine truth. The realms are, or have become, totally foreign to each other. If there is to be communication—revelation—then it can only be at the initiative of the transcendent. (What we today call "natural theology" seems to be at least a practical impossibility in this scheme.) Only those claims that can demonstrate they are based on the divine initiative—have a unique origin in the transcendent—can be trusted. Of course, John knows as well as anyone else that such claims cannot be scientifically proven. Hence he has to stress commitment—"believing in."

For our author ("John"), without such knowledge of the transcendent, which is "light," human life is a lost, meaningless existence—a life in "darkness." True life can exist only in knowing the divine. To know is to participate in the transcendent and the union created in participation is salvation (John's preferred term is "eternal life"). *The ultimate destiny of a human is dependent upon the knowing of the transcendent.*

The author of the Gospel then has his primary task set. John must convince the reader that Jesus Christ has a unique origin in the transcendent in order that the revelation given by the fleshly Jesus be taken as true over against all other competing truth claims. Only in this way can John expect the reader or hearer of the Gospel to commit herself to the truth revealed therein.

If this were his only problem, then John's task would have been simple. An either-or with no exceptions could be set up. He could affirm that Jesus Christ is absolutely the only revelation and all other claims are completely false. Sometimes, in fact, John does seem to suggest this kind of dualism and to be heading in the direction of a Marcion.[10]

The matter, however, is not so simple. Christianity emerged out of Judaism. The Torah is in some sense still honored by John's community, and the final (?) separation between church and synagogue is a recent event, the recalling of which is painful.[11] He cannot and does not really want to deny that the Father of the Son is the God worshiped by the Jews or that the Torah is true at least to the extent that it points to the very truth embodied in Jesus himself (see 5:39). He is not able to ignore the belief that this Father created the cosmos.

Thus John has to qualify the either-or to deal with the revelatory nature of God's relationship with Israel. There are indications that John feels uncomfortable making this concession, yet he stubbornly clings to the need to incorporate, however ambiguously, the truth revealed to Israel within his structure. This also will manifest itself through his telling of the story.

While I have used the terms "transcendent" and "immanent" because they may communicate easily (I have avoided, of course, the philosophical difficulties involved in their use!), these are not the author's own terms. The realm I have pointed to by "transcendent" is for John preeminently the reality of the Father, that ultimate reality shared by Logos, Son, Paraclete (Spirit), and, ultimately, the believer.

The immanent is addressed as "world" and as "flesh." Just as the immanent is not in and of itself negative or evil, so for our author world and flesh have their rightful place as part of the order of God's creation. At the same time, John implies that the world has rebelled and become darkness (1:5). Thus there are two strikes against world and flesh. They are separated from the Father by the order of reality, and they have refused relationship with him, which results in the impossibility of participation in eternal life. Hereafter I will avoid the use of "transcendent" and "immanent" as much as possible and confine myself to those terms used by our author. We must be aware, however, that "Father" and "world" denote two distinctly separate realities, sometimes opposed to each other.

The Choice of the Story Form

With such heady ideas to communicate, one might expect John to choose an abstract treatise form as the best medium for his message. Such forms were, of course, known in the literary world of his day, and he was probably familiar with some of these. The Epistle to the Hebrews indicates such a form could be chosen by Christian authors of the late first century. In fact, a later member of his own community will use the treatise form (1 John, thinly disguised as an epistle).[12]

Instead John chose narrative. To convey his deepest thoughts about eternal reality he writes a story about the earthly Jesus! He was, of course, not the first to tell the story about Jesus, and such stories must have been familiar to him, whether or not he had actually read any of the Synoptics in their present form.[13] We must not be misled, however, into assuming that he used this form just because it was becoming traditional. Since he knew other forms, he must have chosen the narrative form because it seemed the best vehicle for what he wanted to say.

Why did he make this decision? To answer this question may seem—actually is—speculative. I will hazard a guess. It seems to me that the story form actually communicates better his understanding of the revelatory act than does an abstract treatise.

Eternal life is participation in ultimate reality. That reality cannot be captured in, nor participation best elicited by, propositional sentences or theological treatises. Propositions, since they are human language, belong to this world and are flesh. John, of course, inevitably needs human language to write a narrative, but he knows that his language is not to be equated with the reality itself. Language can only point to that truth, hint at it, symbolize it. John's awareness of this chasm between ultimate reality and language must be the reason he depends so heavily on symbols. Symbols and narrative lure one to more than intellectual assent. They evoke commitment.[14]

Even the teaching of Jesus in the Gospel turns out on close inspection to be nonpropositional. The famous conundrum posed by Rudolf Bultmann is on target. Question: Who is Jesus according to the Gospel of John? Answer: He is the revealer. Question: What does he reveal? Answer: He reveals that he is the revealer.[15] That is, there is no substantive content to what Jesus reveals. To say, for example, "I and the Father are One," is to say everything and nothing at the same time.[16]

Thus, given John's structure, an abstract treatise could actually be self-defeating. The reality of the Father cannot be communicated in propositions; it must be experienced. The old adage "Seeing is believing" fairly describes John's viewpoint. In fact, he teases the reader by the challenge: "Come and see!" (1:39; see also 12:21). But what is it that one sees? Instead of propositions or creeds, one sees a person living and acting in the world, a person who ultimately dies on the cross, just at that moment most clearly manifesting "the glory" (a Johannine term for revelation) of the Father. For just as a person is always more than the sum of any set of propositions that could be made about him, so Jesus Christ as person is that which is the appropriate and full revelation of the transcendent. Only as person can he be the perfectly transparent window to the divine reality.

John takes a final, bold step. Just as Jesus does not teach in propositional sentences the reality of the Father, so the person of Jesus on earth does not walk in undisguised divinity. The revelation of God has become flesh. That Jesus was human was an unavoidable affirmation, since it was a given in the tradition, but it would seem to create great difficulties for John's structure. If the reality of the Father is entirely separate from the reality of the flesh, how can the true revelation of the Father take place in and through flesh?

John no more explains this ambiguity or paradox (or is it a self-contradiction?) than anyone in Christian theology has since. His greatness is perhaps his willingness to allow the ambiguity to remain without trying to repress it or ease the tension it creates in him or his reader. There is certainly a tendency toward a docetic (i.e., not human) Jesus in places in the Gospel (the author must have been tempted), but the tendency is restrained.[17] By his bold statement, "The logos became flesh," John states at the very beginning his intention to accept the ultimate ambiguity of the vehicle of revelation.

Acceptance of this ambiguity must have forced the conclusion that a story of the fleshly Jesus was not only an appropriate but, indeed, the best, most holistic vehicle for his purpose. *Only through narrative can he point to the reality of the Father revealed through the ambiguity of flesh.*

Through the centuries the Gospel of John has told this powerful story, long before scholars were able to write about it with the sophistication they do today. To write or read about the Gospel of John is thus no substitute for the experience promised and possible in the reading of the Gospel itself. Let the reader of this book beware! There is even a certain perversity, perhaps, in undertaking an abstract explanation of narrative. I take courage in the fact that nothing said here can destroy the power of the narrative itself, and I strongly urge the reader to take the time to read the Gospel through in a single sitting. In the exposition which follows I shall try as often as possible to show how the ideas fit into the movement of the plot. John tells us what he wants to, when he wants to.[18]

Which John?

The Gospel emerged out of a continuing community which had developed its own distinctive theological and literary style. Almost all scholars agree that several different stages in the community are recognizable and that these are reflected in different strata within the extant literary productions of the community.[19]

We can begin by distinguishing between the Gospel itself and the three epistles—1, 2, and 3 John. It is surely correct to conclude that the author of the Gospel is not the author of these documents.[20] They represent, rather, a later stage of the community after it has split into at least two groups who are now bitterly opposing each other. This means that the epistles cannot be used to interpret the Gospel itself, however much they come from the same community and reflect the same literary style.

More complex is the issue of the integrity of the Gospel (that is, whether the text as we now have it is the very text composed by the original author). There are indications that our canonical Gospel is a modified or edited version of an earlier original.[21] Chapter 21 is generally seen to be a later addition (appendix), the original Gospel ending fittingly at the conclusion of chapter 20. Many scholars believe there have been other additions (notably 6:51b–58) and some transpositions of the original order. Not infrequently researchers make an attempt to reconstruct the original Gospel, attributing the present text to a revision by an editor who had views somewhat different from the original author.

This is a fascinating detective game, and I myself am convinced that there was such an editor, whose ideas not only are different from those of the original author but actually are in some conflict with them. Nevertheless, in this book my task is to interpret the text as it stands, even if that probably means interpreting the "second edition." After all, this edition is in the canon and is the one to which we are ultimately responsible. Fortunately, on specific issues of Christology the two editions do not seem to vary significantly in ideas.

CHAPTER SEVEN

UNITY WITH THE FATHER

High Christology! Jesus Christ is completely divine, is God. This is the judgment universally held of the thought of the Gospel of John. For some people, this is a delightful affirmation. At last we are on the plane of Nicaea. For others, it marks a dark, fateful turn in the road. From now on the genuine humanity of Jesus will become increasingly doubtful and useless.

In a sense both perspectives are correct, if one is looking back on the Gospel from later centuries. To understand the Gospel itself, however, it is imperative to avoid such retrospective glances. Our task is rather to look forward to the Christology of John as a solution to issues and problems that lay behind the actual composition. To comprehend we must ask what compelled the author to reach his conclusions? Why is John so concerned to assert the unity of Son with the Father?

If our proposal in the previous chapter is correct, the solution to this fundamental question is to be found in his felt need to assure the purity, and therefore the validity, of the revelation in Jesus Christ. The bitter conflict between church and synagogue implied in chapters 5—12 indicates that much pain resulted from the extreme christological claims of the community. Clearly John's thought is not an intellectual exercise. It is a statement he feels compelled to make despite the deep rift he sees it causing in his society. Not to sense the painful crucible which shapes his thought is to trivialize his theological affirmations.

Of course, to understand is not the same thing as to agree with. Nor will anyone claim that John's crucible is the same as ours. Nevertheless, out of specific and time-bound situations a profound thinker can reach judgments that transcend her or his time, to become affirmations which need to be heard in other days. Whether the author of the Gospel has reached this level is our ultimate question.

The Plot of the Gospel

Before we explore the various themes John uses to point to the unity of Son with the Father, we need to say something about how he tells his

63

story.[1] The narrative can be divided into three main sections or books.

Book I extends from the beginning of the narrative proper at John 1:19 through chapter 12. In this section Jesus states his case and encounters increasing conflict from his opponents primarily because of what he claims about himself. In these claims and counterclaims are to be found the conflict between the church and synagogue of John's own day. That is, the story moves on two levels. At the surface level the story is about Jesus and his own situation. Below this, however, lies the implied level of John's church. What Jesus says about himself is thus what the Johannine community is saying about Jesus Christ.[2]

Book II consists of chapters 13 through 17. Here Jesus gathers for final discussion with his disciples.[3] Through monologue, dialogue, and prayer Jesus discloses the meaning of discipleship and points to the coming of the Spirit (the Paraclete). He reveals what that means for the church that will emerge after his return to the Father. Again it is obvious that what Jesus says has meaning for the church of John's day.

Book III consists of chapters 18 through 20 containing John's narration of the familiar story of Jesus' arrest, trial, death, and resurrection (the Passion Narrative). Of course John tells it his own way, so that for many early readers what was familiar must have had a decidedly unfamiliar ring to it. Chapter 21 (an appendix to the first edition) can best be taken as an epilogue.

On the surface this plot seems to be chronologically structured. A careful reading, however, shows how superficial the chronology actually is. At a deeper level one sees that the plot is arranged to bring out the various ideas John wants the reader to learn, at the points where he wants them to enter the reader's consciousness. One could call this a theological narrative.

The author, however, does not woodenly say everything in his mind about a given point or reveal completely the depth of a symbol at one place. The first reference may be a hint, an allusion, followed up later by other more direct statements. In one sense this is a developmental scheme, but a development more in the consciousness of the reader than in the thought itself. A perceptive reader at some point midway in the story is bound to exclaim: "Oh, this is what John meant four pages ago!" Some have called this a "spiral" technique, the author returning again and again to a motif, each time expecting a greater awareness on the part of the reader. This is reason enough for us to read the Gospel through in a single sitting.

John's narrative technique can then be seen as one of luring the reader into gradually greater awareness of the truth of Jesus. But if this is so, the prologue (1:1–18) seems problematic. In the prologue the author seems to give it all away before the story even begins! In concepts even more lofty than those encountered in the narrative, the prologue reveals from the standpoint of the reality of the Father (*sub specie aeternitatis*) what the true meaning of the shortly-to-be-told story is. Thus the deductive dynamic of the prologue seems to conflict with the inductive dynamic of the narrative.

Indeed some scholars have suspected that the prologue was a later addition to the original narrative, which must then have begun at 1:19—in which case we would truly have an inductive, almost enigmatic beginning. It is even tempting to describe first the thought as it develops in the narrative and then return to the prologue as a summary. This is, however, obviously not how the early readers (once the prologue was attached, if it was so attached) would have read it.

To be fair to the Gospel, we must read it as it was finally intended to be read and describe it in that order. Thus we must first encounter the prologue and then put the narrative in that context. When the reader starts the plot about the human Jesus, she already knows the plot about the eternal logos. Granted, this context probably takes away something of the surprise and the lure from the narrative. The reader already knows about the logos; as she reads the narrative, she learns how the earthly Jesus belongs to that eternal reality.

The Logos of the Father

Logos means "word." The logos of the Father is the Word of the Father, the speech of God. But what does this mean? Does it mean the proliferation of increasingly meaningless sounds—"Words, words, words"—a sense of surfeit we all experience today? Or can it mean that solemn assertion that word and the truth of the person are the same, as in "you have my word for it"?

For Israelite theologians God's Word was enactment of his power and will. "By the word of the Lord the heavens were made" (Ps. 33:6). "By myself I have sworn, from my mouth has gone forth in righteousness a word that shall not return" (Isa. 45:23). And since God is defined, is known in his enactment, God's Word is self-revelation.

Thus the logos of the Father is the revelation of the Father, a conception the prologue holds in common with the Hebrew Bible. The prologue goes farther. The logos has here a personal identity, a status independent of God without in any way becoming separate from God's reality.

The logos was with God (individuality)
The logos was God (identification)

The paradox which will result in the mystery of the Trinity is here stated for the first time in Christianity.

The various possible influences of religions and philosophies upon John's thought here make an intricate and complex puzzle, which we cannot describe.[4] We must single-mindedly focus upon the function of this paradox in John's Christology. It enables the basic need for the claims of unity with the Father to be met, without absorbing the independent status of the Son into the Father. Were this independence lost, the revelation he brings would not be qualitatively different from other, past acts of the Father narrated in the Torah. John has to have it both ways! The logos must be the same as and yet distinct from the Father in order for its manifestation in the world in Jesus Christ to be the unique revelation of the Father. Preexistence is thus essential to John's theology.

Once this unity and distinctness is established, the prologue can proceed to list the activities of the logos which are at the same time the activities of God. The logos is the creative act by which all the cosmos came into existence. The logos is light and life, that is, the revelatory and salvatory manifestation of God in that created cosmos.

A somber tone is quietly introduced into the brightness of the revelation (1:5). The created cosmos has somehow become darkness, and those belonging to the logos (because they are creatures) reject the revelations (1:11—probably a reference to God's relationship with Israel as recorded in the Torah).[5] While no explanation is given for this rebellion, its reality is affirmed at the beginning of the story, so that later, in the description of the hostility manifested toward Jesus, the reader will not be surprised.

The christological climax comes in vv. 14, 16–18. The logos becomes flesh. "We [the confessing community] have seen his glory, glory as the only begotten from the Father, full of grace and truth"(au. trans.), despite the fact that the logos has assumed the ambiguity of fleshly existence. The reader is confronted here with terms burdened with meaning. "Glory" is a biblical term for revelation. To see the glory of the enfleshed logos is to perceive the true reality of the logos. But since that glory is of the "only begotten" (i.e., the unique manifestation) of the Father, the community confesses that through the enfleshed logos it has seen the revelation of God herself.

That glory is full (or "perfect") of grace and truth. "Grace" is not a word that appears in the Gospel outside of the prologue (just as "logos" will disappear in the precise meaning it has in the prologue). Here "grace" (*charis*) must mean that the revelation of God is a gift to the world. It has to be gift, for the world cannot of itself know or perceive the glory. "Truth"(*alētheia*), on the other hand, is key to John's vocabulary. Truth is the reality of an entity.[6] Here the reality is that of God himself. Thus in every way the prologue hammers home the basic claim: In the enfleshed logos is the unique revelation of God. Only because the logos is both united with and yet distinct from God can the community trust, confess, that in the enfleshed logos one has that very vision of the reality of God which brings eternal life.

Even a reader familiar with this text may be surprised to realize that up to this point this enfleshed logos has not been named. To say the logos became flesh points toward some earthly figure, but who? Verses 6–8 and 15 make it clear that it is not John the Baptist (perhaps rebutting claims by some of his followers that he was). Verse 17 both shows that it was not Moses either and, for the first time, introduces the appropriate name into the text: "The law was given through Moses; grace and truth came through Jesus Christ." The enfleshed logos is none other than Jesus of Nazareth!

Once the logos is named, the prologue reaches its end and christological climax by the most obviously audacious claim of all. "No one has ever seen God; the only begotten God, who is in the bosom of the Father, that one has made him [God] known" (v. 18, au. trans.). Here the author is not speaking simply of the eternal logos before the enfleshment. He proclaims the salvific result: *in this enfleshment the very reality of God is revealed.* The prologue shows as sharply as possible that the ground of this soteriological revelation is the unity of logos with Father and the appearance of this very logos in the flesh of Jesus Christ.

Thus the stage is set. Now the drama must unfold. The same christological point will be pursued relentlessly with varying terms and symbols. The reader now at least knows what to be looking for and how to interpret the hints and often veiled statements that will be presented to her.

Having this perspective will also free us from the necessity of following the plot "straight through" (a rewarding and fascinating task on its own). We can limit our focus to those motifs and symbols which further perception of John's primary christological concern. We will, however, follow those motifs as they are progressively unveiled by the plot movement. And, exactly contrary to the approach I used to uncover Paul's Christology, the titles become a crucial thematic—but not the titles in and of themselves! Rather, it is through the way John molds and manipulates the traditional titles that our understanding is deepened.

The Son

Statistics are sometimes revealing. Here are some that are! In the Gospel, the primary term for divine reality is "Father" (*pater*), not "God." About 120 times "Father" is used to refer to this reality, while God (*theos*) is used only about 75. This is a greater frequency than that in any of the other Gospels and off the chart in comparison with Paul.

A correlate set of statistics involves the titles used of Jesus. *Christos* and *messiah* (i.e., the Hebrew term transliterated into Greek) appear only about 17 times, and some of these appearances are ambiguous and not directly titular of Jesus. *Kyrios* (Lord) appears 14 times not in the vocative (a situation in which the meaning is ambiguous), and 9 of these nonvocative occurrences are in the narratives about the resurrected Jesus. The designation "prophet" occurs but a few times. Perhaps surprisingly, the author is often content to use the simple name "Jesus" which occurs more often in John's Gospel than in any of the others.

The clearly preferred title is "Son" (39 times). The obvious correlation, Father/Son, immediately suggests itself. The picture, however, is not simple. At times Jesus is called "Son of God" (9 times), sometimes "Son of man" (12 times), and most often simply "Son" or "the Son" (18 times). Each set has to be investigated independently, although there are sometimes important overlaps.

In one important respect, John uses the sets consistently. Of the 39 appearances, 33 occur in Book I, while only 4 appear in Book II, the discourse which Jesus holds with his disciples. Even within Book I, the majority (28) are bunched into the first eight chapters, only 5 appearing in chapters 9—12. That is, the author of the Gospel uses the "Son" epithet primarily in the beginning controversy chapters and not in "intra church" discourse. It functions *in conflict settings* and thus must reflect arguments about titles between John's community and the synagogue.

Son of God. Most of the occurrences of this full title show that the title is primarily one of confession. When a person wants to acknowledge faith in Jesus, or to the contrary, when one wants to reject such faith, this title is likely to occur. John the Baptist and Nathanael both confess Jesus to be Son of God in the first chapter, and the original edition of the Gospel ended at 20:31 with the words: "That you may believe that Jesus is the Christ, the Son of God, and that believing you may have life in his name." In 19:7 the Jews want Jesus to be executed "because he has made himself the Son of God." Since the title is used traditionally as confession, I do not think it possible to deduce much about John's Christology from it. It is perhaps not unimportant to note that only 2 of these 9 (5:25 and 10:36) contain the correlate image of "Father."

The Son. These 18 occurrences do, I believe, show us the distinctive value John sees in the title. They are not confessional in character and thus reflect directly John's own thinking. Virtually all of them directly correlate Son with God as Father, and the few that do not have Father in the same sentence have this designation in an adjacent sentence. The apparent exception is the crucial passage, 3:16–17, where John writes: "For God so loved the world that he gave his only Son," followed by the next sentence: "For

God sent the Son into the world. . . ." This exception, I would suggest, is only apparent because the phrase, "his only Son," demands an implied "Father" as subject.

The most important conclusion about John's use of "Son" is already given by this brief analysis. He wants to correlate as closely as possible Son with Father. Just as "Father" is for him the most adequate designation of divine reality, so "Son" is that which most appropriately discloses the meaning of Jesus Christ. Indeed, they must be understood together, virtually as one concept.

And why? I would suggest that through this correlation John wants to point to the intimacy of the relation of Father and Son. This intimacy implies the union of the two and provides another assurance of the divine reality in Jesus. In 5:19, we read, "The Son can do nothing of his own accord, but only what he sees the Father doing" (cf. pp. 78–80). While this sentence may be a short parable taken from the imagery of work-apprenticeship, the application to the unity of the divine reality in Father and Son will be made clear in succeeding sentences. If the Son does only what he sees the Father doing, then the Son is a complete revelation of the will of the Father.[7]

Postbiblical theologians, influenced by substance-oriented concepts of God, will use John to prove the substantival unity of God and Christ, Father and Son. If John had thought substantivally of divine reality, I doubt he would have objected to this use. John's own purpose, however, must be distinguished from that of the later theologians. For John, the function of Jesus as "Son" is to show such an intimate union with the Father that only Jesus as Son can be claimed as the perfect revelation of the divine reality. "I and the Father are one" means that one can only know the Father through the Son.[8]

Son of Man. This title, known to us from its frequent appearance in the Synoptics, functions in John in ways distinct from the titles discussed above. The problems of origin and Jewish background of the title are serious ones, but we cannot discuss them here.[9] I think it fair to say simply that the Synoptic evidence indicates that the phrase is titular in early Christianity, and that functions of eschatological judgment and leadership of the elect are attached to it in the earliest stratum of Christian tradition (as they are also in *1 Enoch*). John, or the tradition upon which he is dependent, has bent this early tradition in ways consonant with his own christological needs. In some ways this pre-Johannine Christian tradition shines through the new functions John has assigned the title. It may even be that the association of the title with the death of Jesus, evidenced in Mark, was known to the Johannine community.

There are two main clusters of meaning attached to the Son of man in the Gospel: (1) *The descending-ascending motif.* John's christological structure has often been called that of the descending-ascending savior. Given belief in the preexistence and resurrection of Jesus, there is something obvious about such a scheme. John, however, stresses this "movement" and identifies it with the Son of man title. (2) *The cross-exaltation theme.* John's working of this theme is unique in early Christian literature; yet it is spiritually akin to the Markan idea of the suffering Son of man. Both Johannine themes are interwoven because they function in a similar way: to ensure the validity of the revelation in Jesus Christ.

The first appearance of the title occurs in enigmatic fashion in 1:51, as the climax to a section in which all the titles John uses in the narrative are by one person or another ascribed to Jesus. It is Jesus himself, however, who speaks of the Son of man. "Truly, truly, I say to you, you will see heaven opened, and the angels of God ascending and descending upon the Son of man." The passage is actually not as opaque as it may seem, and the interested reader can consult the commentaries for explanation.

Suffice it to say for our purposes that the descending-ascending motif is linked with the title; here, however, it is not the Son of man who "moves" but the angels, while the Son of man takes the place of the ladder in Jacob's dream (the basis of the Johannine imagery). The point, it is generally agreed, is that Jesus is the vehicle of communication between heaven and earth. Already at this early stage of the story, there is a hint that Son of man is related to the issue of revelation. That hint will be repeated with greater clarity in the next occurrence of the title in John 3:13-14:

> No one has ascended into heaven but he who descended from heaven, the Son of man. And as Moses lifted up the serpent in the wilderness, so must the Son of man be lifted up, that whoever believes in him may have eternal life.

Here it is clear that it is the Son of man who descends and ascends, in implied distinction from all other claimants of ascent, that is, of apocalyptic revealers of heavenly knowledge. If the Son of man has descended, it means he comes from God and thus is uniquely able to be the revealer of God. The reader will already know, of course, that the descending Son of man is the same as the logos who has the status of God.

The next sentence, however, seems to move to a different motif, at least to a different metaphor. The reference to Moses recalls the story in Num. 21:4-9. As punishment God has sent poisonous serpents to afflict the Israelites. The people repent, so God instructs Moses to make a bronze serpent, attach it to a pole, and lift it up in the air so that people can look on it. All those bitten who looked upon the serpent were saved from death. Analogously the Son of man must be lifted up so that he may save others from death, to have eternal life. But what does "lifted up" mean? Those who have read the entire Gospel (in Greek) will look back at this passage and remark upon the author's ability to create a triple-entendre (John has already created two double-entendres in the previous verses!). For in Greek, the verb can mean either a physical raising or a metaphorical raising, in the sense of exaltation. It is almost certain that there are three levels here. The first is the physical level of the crucifixion, in which Jesus is raised above ground on the cross. The second is the metaphorical meaning of exaltation, for John will make it clear that the cross is the moment of exaltation, not that of greatest degradation. There is probably a third level, that of resurrection—the ultimate raising. In John cross and resurrection are closely connected.

Salvador Dali's painting of the crucifixion, "The Christ of St. John of the Cross," visually captures this layered meaning in a haunting way. The viewer is looking down on Jesus' crucifixion, and yet the cross itself is elevated far above the ground. Jesus on the cross is being "lifted up" to heaven.

This new motif is not, however, ultimately separate in function from that of descending-ascending. The first-time reader cannot yet know, but will later learn, that the cross-exaltation is exactly that supreme moment of revelation, of greatest glorification of the Father. The implication is that those who "see" (believe in) Jesus as he is lifted up (exalted) will have eternal life. Why? Because in this moment they see God the Father most clearly.

The reader realizes the central function of the title when he arrives at John 12:20–36, that section in which Jesus most fully explains the significance of his death. The main thematic here is the glorification of Father and Son (see p. 73 below). The title "Son of man" is, however, interwoven into that motif.

The appearance of Greeks who want to "see Jesus" prompts Jesus to exclaim: "The hour has come for the Son of man to be glorified" (12:23). The reader knows by now that the hour is the crucifixion but should suspect that it is the eschatological hour as well. The converging of revelational motifs on the moment of death is intense.

This intensity is increased a few sentences later when Jesus says: "And I, when I am lifted up from the earth, will draw all people to myself" (12:32, au. trans.). The verb "lifted up" is, of course, the same as in 3:14, but Jesus has used the first-person pronoun rather than the title to speak of himself. John cleverly has the crowd supply the title and thus remind the reader: "We have heard from the law that the Christ remains for ever. How can you say that the Son of man must be lifted up? Who is this Son of man?" (12:34). Of course Jesus has not said that the Son of man must be lifted up, but the reader should already have made the association.

The final occurrence of the title is in the opening scenes of the final discourses. Judas finally separates himself from the inner group. After Judas has left to fulfill the deed of betrayal, Jesus says: "Now is the Son of man glorified, and in him God is glorified" (13:31). Here reference to descent-ascent as well as lifting up is absent; a link is made only to the theme of glorification (i.e., also revelation; cf. p. 73 below). This final use of the title makes the entire sequence transparent: the Son of man is the revelation of the divine reality.[10]

Summary. It is fascinating to see how the author of the Gospel of John uses both "Son" thematics—Son of the Father and Son of man—for ultimately the same purpose: to show how Jesus Christ can be the true revelation of divine reality. This is especially interesting since each thematic has distinct contours and with one exception the author keeps these contours discrete.[11]

Glory

In Israelite theology, God cannot be seen. Yet the seer, paradoxically, sees something of the divine. Since it could not be God himself, a term was needed to point to what could be seen even if it could not be seen. This term was *kavōd*, translated in the Septuagint by *doxa*. The straining at the linguistic and conceptual barriers is clear from Ezek. 1:28. After the prophet has "seen" the chariot of God, he concludes: "Such was the appearance of the likeness of the glory [*kavōd*] of the Lord."

While God cannot be seen, her glory can. Thus God's glory is what can be known of the divine, that is, is the revelation of God. It is this meaning John picks up and uses frequently in his program of pointing to Jesus Christ as the revelation of God. At first reading, the profusion of apparently different sorts of glorification is confusing. God is glorified; Jesus is glorified; Jesus glorifies God; God glorifies Jesus. Glorification is past and yet future. It is, however, precisely the mutual glorification of Father and Son that is the point. A few examples must suffice.

Already in the prologue the theme is introduced. The community confesses that in the enfleshed logos it beholds glory, "Glory as the only begotten from the Father" (1:14, au. trans.). The glory of the logos is not independent of the Father. Indeed, he has this glory only because he is the "only begotten from the Father."

Yet the next mention of Jesus' glory does seem to give it a reality independent of the Father. As the conclusion to the miracle at Cana, the author writes: "This, the first of his signs, Jesus did at Cana in Galilee, and manifested his glory; and his disciples believed in him" (2:11). Jesus seems to be portrayed here as the powerful "divine man" who can perform miracles over nature, turning water into wine. In fact, the miracle as manifestation of glory leads the disciples to believe in him.[12]

Three passages, however, occurring later in the Gospel make clear to the reader a deeper level of John's thought.

1. We have already pointed to chapter 12 as the place where the meaning of Jesus' death becomes clarified. The theme of glory is prominent here. Speaking of his impending execution Jesus says: "The hour has come for the Son of man to be glorified" (12:23). Death is glorification! Jesus' death is somehow the revelation of God. This becomes explicit a few sentences later when, again speaking of the hour of his death, Jesus speaks to his Father: "Father, glorify thy name" (12:28). This could be paraphrased: Father, reveal thy reality. The divine voice speaks in response: "I have glorified it, and I will glorify it again." Clearly the glorification has taken, and will take place in Jesus, the future pointing to what lies ahead in the narrative, probably both death and resurrection. Thus the revelation of God is said by God himself to have its locus in Jesus on earth.

2. A similar affirmation occurs in chapter 13 after Judas leaves the company of disciples. "Now is the Son of man glorified, and in him God is glorified" (13:31). The mutuality which points to the revelation of God in the person of Jesus is explicit. Then follows an awkward sentence as it stands in many texts (there may be a copyist's error behind this awkwardness). "If [since] God is glorified in him, God will also glorify him in himself, and glorify him at once" (13:32). Here the past of Jesus is God's glorification, but also the future, and an immediate future ("at once"). The emphasis seems to be on that future which includes death and resurrection.

3. Finally we can point to the "high-priestly prayer" in chapter 17, where again the theme of glory is prominent. "Father, the hour has come; glorify thy Son that the Son may glorify thee" (17:1). The mutuality of glorification is by now familiar to the reader. But in v. 5 something new is said. Jesus prays: "Father, glorify thou me in thy own presence with the glory which I had with thee before the world was made." Glory is now shown to be eternal, stretching from the preexistence of the logos to the return to that heavenly realm by the resurrected Jesus. This request is not self-gratification, for Jesus then prays that the believers may behold that eternal glory (17:24). Mutual glorification is both participation in ultimate reality and the revelation of that reality. Since to see is to participate, the believer is promised a sharing in that reality itself.

The motif of glorification thus functions in the Gospel, as does the title "Son," to insist upon the validity of the divine revelation in Christ. It is as both Son of man (12:23; 13:31) and Son of the Father (17:1) that Jesus is glorified, is thus the unique revealer of God.

Epiphany Formulas

Briefly, and finally, one needs to notice the various "I am" statements that Jesus makes repeatedly in his discourses. This very simple linguistic device (a statement by a divine being manifesting his or her power), has been found in both Hellenistic and Hebraic sources.[13] An ironic twist to such an epiphanic statement occurs in the narration of Jesus' arrest. When the posse confronts Jesus, he asks the officers whom they want. When they reply that they seek Jesus of Nazareth, Jesus replies simply, "I am [he]" (*egō eimi*, au. trans.). John reports that when they heard this "they drew back and fell to the ground" (18:6). The question and answer is repeated, and this time the posse arrests him. This little imaginative interruption into an otherwise realistic narrative is intended as a delicious remark to the "insiders." Even the enemies of Jesus must fall to the ground before the manifestation of divinity.

Most of the time, however, the "I am" formulas have a predicate, and the formulaic importance can be lost in the sentence. We should not forget, however, that they remain epiphanic. The first instance in the narrative (here, nonpredicative) occurs in response to the Samaritan woman's statement about the Messiah. Jesus responds: "I am, who is speaking to you" (4:26, au. trans.). In 6:35 Jesus says, "I am the bread of life." In 8:12: "I am the light of the world." "Before Abraham was, I am" (8:58). "I am the good shepherd" (10:11). "I am the resurrection and the life" (11:25). "I am the way, and the truth, and the life" (14:6).

These few examples show that John delights in such formulas. As epiphanies of the divine, they show that Jesus belongs to the divine reality and point to the soteriological result of that participation. Yet in general these are discreetly kept separate from the other means by which unity with the divine reality is asserted. John does not have Jesus say, "I am the Son," "I am the Son of man." Perhaps the climactic and summary formula is the last one cited: "I am the way, and the truth, and the life." As "way" he is the access to divine reality; as "truth" he is that reality itself; as "life" he is the bestower of salvation.

What Is the Divine Reality?

By now it should be clear: John hammers away almost monotonously at the theme of unity of Father and Son, using various means to keep in the reader's consciousness his basic purpose. But does this not all result in a gigantic tautology? If all Jesus reveals is that he is the revealer, what is the point of it? What do we learn about God? Apparently nothing!

To these natural and pressing questions two things, I think, must be said. First, to be true to John we must hold to the tautology. The reality of God is not adequately contained in words, biblical passages, creeds. God must be experienced, "seen" rather than read about. If that is true for God, it is equally true for any source of revelation. That means the author of the Gospel to be true to his perspective cannot try to capture the meaning of Jesus in statements, creeds, or formulas. As already suggested, words belong to the reality of this world. What humans must know lies in that realm to which words can only point.

This is, of course, one way of stating the *via negativa,* the awareness that in the face of the transcendent one can really only say what it is not. And yet, paradoxically, something crucially positive has been affirmed through all the negatives. Bultmann himself is aware of this "other side" and states it powerfully. Revelation contains within itself "the shattering and negating of all human self-assertion and all human norms and evaluations. And, precisely by virtue of being such negation, the Revelation is the affirmation and fulfillment of human longing for life, for true reality."[14]

While nothing must dilute the stark truth of this *via negativa,* a *second* statement must also be affirmed. There is, indeed, one word that John thinks most adequately points to the unutterable reality, and that one word is *agapē,* love. Granted, it is not John who says, "God is love." That assertion is made, rather, by 1 John (4:8). In many places 1 John wishes to move in the direction of credal formulas, a tendency John's Gospel steadfastly avoided. For John there is no predicate that is exhaustive of God's reality.

There is no word and yet there is a word—*love.* This paradox must be maintained, but it has to be acknowledged that the author has chosen as his one word the trickiest, most ambiguous word possible! Into this word we pour anything we desire. Anybody who looks deeply into the human psyche knows that it can even mask hatred. Is, then, his choice of love as *the* word part of his gigantic tautology?

I think not, because he is careful to show what action he means by the word (statistically he much prefers the verb to the noun). "To love" means an act of willing giving for another, an act which may end in the giving up of one's self.

Let us follow the author's unfolding of his interpretation. The term "to love" does not occur until 3:16, that famous sentence which to many people (perhaps correctly) sums up the meaning of the Gospel: "For God so loved the world that he gave his only son . . ." The next verse affirms that God *sent* his son so that the world might be saved. "Giving" can be a sacrificial term, but John does not really have a cultic view of Jesus' death, and the sending language of the following verse turns the metaphor away from the sacrificial.[15] It is true that the preceding verses (3:14–15—on which our passage may be a comment) do refer to the death, but, as we have seen, they point to revelation, not sacrifice. This should be sufficient to make us reject the metaphor of cultic sacrifice as the clue to God's love in the Gospel.

Another approach may be more fruitful. "For God so loved the world . . ." I would suggest that this statement *in itself* is remarkable. God cares for the very world which has rebelled against him and preferred darkness to his light. That statement may even have startled the reader, whether Gentile or Jew.

Gods and goddesses could live in splendid detachment from concern for the human world. Their beneficence toward people was believed to be sporadic and mostly unpredictable. True, by our period deities like Isis and Asclepius were praised for their power and willingness to intervene on behalf of some humans in need. One can even speak of divine *philanthropia*. Nevertheless, that God loves the entire cosmos in the way John wishes to affirm is not a usual belief.[16]

Even in Judaism, despite the fact that Yahweh is honored as cosmic creator, such an affirmation is rare. That God loves Israel is powerfully stated. Apart from the implications of a few prophetic passages, however, rarely is God's present love for the entire human race visible in the literature. Apocalyptic and emerging rabbinic thought is, if anything, even less likely to include "the world" within God's saving care.

John 3:16 claims, to the contrary, that God's love is directed toward the entire cosmos for the purpose of salvation, of eternal life. God acts, goes outside of himself, even to the giving and sending of his Son. In giving his Son he gives himself. This act of giving for the sake of the cosmos is as close as one can get to saying what God is.

But since the Son is revelatory of the Father, the *agapē* of the Father must be manifested in the Son, and indeed it is. The first verse of Book II strikes this thematic: "Having loved his own who were in the world, he loved them to the end" (or perhaps "completely"—the Greek is ambiguous—13:1).

Just as in the themes of revelation, the lines of Jesus' love converge on the death. "I am the good shepherd. The good shepherd lays down his life for the sheep" (10:11). In a sentence which points to the death as exemplary of Jesus' care and as a model for his followers, he says: "He who loves his life loses it, and he who hates his life in this world will keep it for eternal life" (12:25).

In the final discourse he says to the disciples: "A new commandment I give to you, that you love one another; even as I have loved you, that you also love one another" (13:34). The context ("Now is the Son of man glorified") makes it clear that the love of Jesus refers to his death. The commandment is repeated in 15:12, followed by the clarifying phrase: "Greater love has no one than this, that one lay down his life for his friends" (15:13, au. trans.).

The convergence of love with death and glorification is, of course, not accidental. Jesus' self-giving unto death is the clearest revelation of God and is thus the glorification of God. Ultimately love by God and the love by Jesus are identical. Hence in the death both God and Jesus are glorified, both are revealed.

Tension is inevitable just at this point. The conflict with outsiders, the dualistic and sectarian tendencies visible in the Gospel (a result of the conflict?) all have led to a sense of the practical limitation of this love for the cosmos. Only those who believe are granted eternal life; Jesus' love seems to be limited to "his own" (13:1), "his friends" (15:13). The disciples are exhorted to "love one another," which must refer to love within, not without the community of believers. And in the final prayer, Jesus excludes the cosmos from his realm of concern; he prays only "for those whom thou hast given me" (17:9). Scholars have noted this and, indeed, complained about the ingrown nature of the *agapē*.[17] (It seems a far cry from Jesus' exhortation in "Q" to love one's enemies.)

All this is true and needs to be acknowledged. It is crucial, nevertheless, to note John's intent, which he clearly enunciates the first time *agapē* is mentioned. God loves the world; God does not intend the condemnation but the salvation of the world. Those who refuse to come to the light bring condemnation upon themselves. That the effect of God's universal love is not universal in fact is then not to be attributed to a limitation of God's care.[18]

God cares! God shows care by the act of self-giving, in sending his Son for the salvation of humankind. The self-giving of the Son, made most visible in the death, is what most clearly reveals this caring. This same self-giving also becomes the model for the lives of those who believe in the Son, so that they may participate in that self-giving love. It is this series of interlocking actions (ultimately one act) which qualifies the strict tautology of the revelation. Unity with the Father is unity of act, of loving. Even so, this love must be seen, accepted, experienced, and participated in to be known and lived.

CHAPTER EIGHT

PROBLEMS IN
JOHN'S CHRISTOLOGY:
OBJECTIONS AND RESPONSES

To say that John's Christology of unity with the Father creates problems is not to demean his thinking or experience. I suppose that any theology worth considering has both logical and existential difficulties. Quite obviously his assertions were going to clash with Jewish theological sensitivities, and one exciting feature of the Gospel is that this clash is made visible in the confrontations of Jesus with his Jewish opponents. Thus we can see what judgments were made against John's Christology and (for our purposes even more importantly) how John handled the objections and incorporated his response to them into his christological affirmations themselves. As with any truly great theologian, John seems to have learned from his opponents. Here I will explore two serious objections raised against his views of Jesus Christ.

The Problem of Ditheism

The more Jesus Christ is elevated toward being one with God, the more the talk sounds like a second god is being installed in the heavens. This problem easily, perhaps inevitably, arises: How to deal with it has exercised the subtleties of all Christian theologians who have struggled with issues of the trinity. For ex-pagans such language may not have been at all disturbing, and even the Samaritan Christian Justin can name Jesus a "second God" without flinching.

For Jews who held their monotheism strictly, however, John's Christology had to be disturbing and offensive. Because of their pagan surroundings, they had to be constantly on guard against polytheistic inroads into their theology. How dangerous must have seemed the movement of the Johannine community—especially as it was initially an intra-Jewish sect—toward a view which in orthodox eyes could only be interpreted as polytheism sneaking in the back door. There are rabbinic texts which darkly oppose unnamed heretics who believe there are "two powers in heaven." Some of the heretics included under this umbrella term were certainly Christians, especially those who moved in the direction John took.[1]

In the Gospel real controversy between Jesus and the Jews does not begin until chapter 5, and it is indicative of the importance of the issue that this initial clash deals precisely with the charge of ditheism. The chapter begins with a healing miracle, which takes place on the Sabbath. To the opponents accosting him "because he did this on the sabbath" (v. 16), Jesus obliquely replies with a metaphor apparently taken from trade apprenticeship: "My Father is working still, and I am working" (v. 17). In what at this point seems like an inappropriate overresponse (due in part to theological shorthand) John comments: "The Jews sought all the more to kill him, because he not only broke the sabbath but also called God his own Father, making himself equal (*isos*) with God" (v. 18).

To translate the shorthand would be too cumbersome here. Suffice it to say that the issue involves a Jewish debate, whether or not God works on the Sabbath (after all, according to Gen. 2:3 he did not). With the assertion that the Father (read "God") does indeed work (on the Sabbath) and "I" (read Jesus) work as well, Jesus claims to be doing the same thing as God does, hence making himself equal to God. John skips over the elaborate steps in the argument, which he assumes his readers will know. As quickly as possible he wishes to get to the accusation: Jesus has made himself to be God. Johannine Christology results in ditheism!

John's response to this charge is a marvelous tour de force, but whether it satisfied the objectors is doubtful. Jesus begins by continuing the metaphor of the apprenticeship. "Truly, truly, I say to you, the son can do nothing of his own accord, but only what he sees the father doing; for whatever he does, that the son does likewise" (5:19). It was customary in ancient societies for a father to teach the son his own trade. The son was in effect an apprentice to his father and learned by imitating the skill of his father. He was, in fact, to do nothing except what he saw his father doing.

If we capitalize the nouns in v. 19, however, the sentence is transformed into a startling christological claim. Jesus is completely subordinate to God. Indeed, Jesus really has no independent will, since his every act, his every volition, is but a copy of what God does. Verse 30 expresses the matter even more clearly: "I can do nothing on my own authority; as I hear, I judge; and my judgment is just, because I seek not my own will but the will of him who sent me."

This means that Jesus is so perfectly a mirror of God that he really has no independent existence. But the converse holds: if Jesus is perfectly a mirror of God, if he does only what God is doing, if he wills only what God wills, then he is the very act and will of God himself! *Complete subordination means complete equality!* Yet the Son's acts of judgment and salvation are not acts of a second god, but of God himself. True, the Son saves and judges "whom he wills" (vv. 21–22), but since the will of the Son is identical with that of the Father, "whom he [the Son] wills" is nothing but "whom the Father wills."

Is it too bold to suggest that this is the first step of Trinitarian reflection in the history of Christian thought? Under pressure from strict monotheistic opponents (some of whom may have been not only unbelieving Jews but also Christians with a different Christology), the author is forced to attempt to preserve monotheism at the same time he struggles to affirm exclusivistic judgments about Jesus Christ which push toward claims for Jesus' divinity.

The conclusion that complete subordination means complete equality is a profound statement, it seems to me, of internal unity of will expressed in external separation. What is particularly interesting about this thinking is that it takes place completely within Jewish understandings of God as will and act, not in terms of later substantival philosophical speculation.

Jesus' Earthly Credentials

John's Christology provided another easy target for Jewish theologians. If Jesus is the enfleshed logos, then he is human. If human, then his status ought to be able to be ascertained by certain credentials, or should it? John himself is not hesitant to use the Hebrew term "Messiah" very early in the narrative (1:41), however inadequately this title may reflect his larger christological picture. But if John is going to have Jesus affirmed as Messiah, then he has a certain responsibility to show that Jesus "looked like" a Messiah the Jewish community could recognize. This he fails to do and it is not surprising that in the story the Jews make strong objections to Jesus because he lacks these credentials. I again assume that the narrative reflects actual debate between the Johannine churches and the synagogue.

Philip says to Nathanael: "We have found him of whom Moses in the law and also the prophets wrote, Jesus of Nazareth, the son of Joseph" (1:45). Notice what is not said: Jesus is not from Bethlehem and he is not son of David. Is it surprising that Nathanael retorts: "Can anything good come out of Nazareth?" Not only does Jesus not come from the proper place to be the Messiah, he comes, so the slur is usually interpreted, from a backward place where no sort of real religious leader could emerge.

Other derogatory statements about his credentials heap up as the controversy heats up. Most of these are concentrated in chapter 7, a section which vividly pictures the Jewish community divided among itself—people against people, people against leaders—over the issue of the meaning of Jesus. He has no formal education, although he "knows letters" (7:15, au. trans.). He is insane (7:20—he has a demon; also 8:48 and 10:20). Not only is Jesus possessed, he is a Samaritan (8:48—probably a slur rather than a statement of believed fact). His pedigree is worthless. "We know where this man comes from; and when the Christ appears, no one will know where he comes from" (7:27). Finally in 7:41–42, the specific charge is made that Jesus' Galilean location disqualifies him, since the credentials of the Messiah mean that he must come from Bethlehem and be descended from David. On the other hand, as all know from the silence of Scripture, "No prophet is to rise from Galilee" (7:52). A kind of ad hominem judgment is even made. The religious leaders—people who are somebody—do not believe in him. Only those do who belong to the ignorant masses, "Who do not know the law" (7:48–49).

Through his Christology of the enfleshed logos John has thus caused objections to rise about the earthly level as well as about the divine. Had he been content to affirm that the revelation has only a divine dimension, he could at least have been spared this problem. That, as we have suggested, was not really an option, given the traditional assumptions in the church of Jesus' humanity. Thus the author has to accept the objections and deal with them as best he can. How does he handle the problem?

Credentials Are Meaningless

First, and very important, John does not try to blunt the accusations. The statements by his opponents are allowed to stand without rebuttal. While the church early on identified Jesus with the tradition that the Messiah must be a son of David (e.g., Rom. 1:3), John does not think it important or possible to make the claim. He does not care to relate Jesus in any way to Bethlehem (as is done in the Matthean and Lukan birth narratives). He does not try to prove that Jesus is educated. Arguments from Scripture are left to stand on their own merit or demerit.

Even the most frequent claim, that he is possessed by a demon, is not really rebutted. The first time, Jesus ignores the charge, on the surface at least (7:20–24). In the second occurrence (8:48–49) Jesus simply says the opposite, while in the third (10:19–21) John has others of the "crowd" reject the accusation, without resolving the conflict.

The most subtle response of all, however, hints at John's position. When Nathanael questions, "Can anything good come out of Nazareth?" Philip simply replies, "Come and see" (1:46). Outside credentials decide nothing. One must "come and see," that is, look at the reality itself, experience what is happening in the event and draw the appropriate conclusions. This is tantamount to rejecting the validity of arguments based on predetermined judgments. John does not care to defend Jesus at this level because the arguments are meaningless to him.

Appeal to Miracles

But the positive side of "Come and see" is that there is indeed something to "see," and John, with his intent to portray Jesus as human, does not ignore all of the "human" manifestations. At this point the issue of the miracles, or "signs" (*semeiai*) as John calls them, emerges. This has presented difficulties in interpretation because the author seems to have an ambiguous attitude toward the signs. They obviously play a positive role in John's claims about Jesus; yet most scholars agree that the author suggests there is also something inadequate about claims for Jesus based solely on them.[2]

John nevertheless allows the signs their place, and thus they are one of the colors in his christological portrait. The signs are a manifestation of Jesus' glory (2:11). The people ask for a sign that they may believe in him (6:30), a request Jesus refuses. Later, others are said to believe in him because of the signs (7:31—see also 9:16 and 10:21). In fact, the conclusion to the original Gospel (20:30–31) seems to emphasize the importance of the signs as a basis for faith.

The most extended treatment of the issue takes place in a heated debate, with the Jews already so angry they are ready to stone him (10:31–39). Jesus retorts: "I have shown you many good works from the Father; for which of these do you stone me?" (v. 32). Here "good works" must refer to miracles. The response is that it is his words, not his works, that are evil. They are blasphemy. Jesus then appeals to his works. "If I am not doing the works of my Father, then do not believe me; but if I do them, even though you do not believe me, believe the works, that you may know and understand that the Father is in me and I am in the Father" (vv. 37–38).

The argument seems to be that belief in the signs ought to lead beyond acceptance of Jesus as wonderworker to belief in his true reality—his unity with the Father. Because signs can lead to a deeper apprehension, John appeals to them. In this narrative, however, his opponents ignore his argument and try to arrest him, seemingly having forgotten that they have stones in their hands!

At any rate signs or miracles have a status beyond that of messianic credentials. Jesus has turned water to wine, made the blind to see, brought the dead to life. These are "signs" which should lead one to reflect on the significance of the man Jesus, to ponder what they might mean, to open the eyes to know who he is.

Irony

The approach that seems most to delight the author is one of irony—in this case professed knowledge which is really ignorance.[3] The Jews know where Jesus has come from. They know his parentage (6:42), that he has come from Galilee (7:52). This claim is summed up in 7:27: "Yet we know where this man comes from; and when the Christ appears, no one will know where he comes from."

The irony is that John and the readers know that the opponents do not know where Jesus has come from, since he really comes from the world of the Father. Jesus responds: "You know me, and you know where I come from? [The Greek is not unambiguously a question, but the RSV by taking it as question captures the irony.] But I have not come of my own accord; he who sent me is true, and him you do not know" (7:28). Hence, if they do not know who sent Jesus, they cannot know whence he has come.

A similar appeal to the source of Jesus' teaching has been made earlier in this same episode. The Jews "marvel" that Jesus "has learning, when he has never studied" (7:15). Jesus replies: "My teaching is not mine, but his who sent me" (v. 16). The teaching comes from above, from the realm of the Father, and is about that realm.

What seems to be a diametrically opposed statement by the Jews on closer look turns out to be explicable in terms of the same irony. In the marvelous vignette of the debate between Jewish leaders and the blind man who has been healed (9:24–34), the authorities say at one point: "We know that God has spoken to Moses, but as for this man, we do not know where he comes from" (v. 29). The statement, from the Johannine perspective, is true; the Jews actually do not know his origin. The leaders, however, intend one meaning in their statement; the reader of the Gospel understands it at a deeper level.

The healed man does not cower before these authorities. In fact he proceeds to lecture them and comes up with the basically right answer as to Jesus' origins: "If this man were not from God, he could do nothing" (v. 33). The man's premise, however, is the miracle of healing: "Never since the world began has it been heard that any one opened the eyes of a man born blind" (v. 32). This shows that for John signs or miracles can lead to right affirmation, although the healed man's final acclamation ("Lord, I believe") comes only after a later encounter with Jesus himself (9:38).

Conclusion

Jesus is indeed human. He lacks the credentials that the Jews think he must have to be the Messiah, but for John that is unimportant. Jesus' signs do, or should, point the way to an understanding that he "is from God." At the deepest level, however, there is no adequate earthly proof or demonstration. The outsiders simply cannot grasp the truth while the insiders already know it.[4] Claim and counterclaim! Where does it get John? One senses that the Johannine community did not do very well in this debate. Jesus cannot produce credentials. He is not the only miracle worker of the day. The use of irony may be humorous for insiders, but it wins no debates with outsiders.

John has been forced to retreat into the ambiguity of history. From historical facts it is impossible to prove metaphysical Truth. When all has been said, flesh retains its finiteness. The claimed transparency of the enfleshed logos ("He who has seen me has seen the Father," 14:9) is stubbornly opaque to the world.

But even though the author of the Gospel may have been forced to this conclusion, he has reached a point that is profoundly insightful. He has become aware that claims and counterclaims about divine reality based on historical "fact" are worthless, whether mounted by Christians or their opponents. This is so because such arguments are inevitably ruled by the criteria of what the world considers important and valid.

True, the logos has, he believes, become enfleshed in Jesus of Nazareth. Jesus lives his life, however, by criteria contrary to that acceptable to the world. Thus the history of Jesus is not only ambiguous, it is, as Rudolf Bultmann has shown, always an offense.

> This offense lies in the fact that the Revealer appears as a man whose claim to be the Son of God is one which he cannot, indeed, must not, prove to the world. For the Revelation is judgment upon the world and is necessarily felt as an attack upon it and an offense to it, so long as the world refuses to give up its norms.[5]

CHAPTER NINE

THE PARACLETE: THE LIGHT
CONTINUES TO SHINE

Jesus is the light of the world. "The light shines in the darkness, and the darkness has not overcome it" (John 1:5). But Jesus leaves the world to return to the Father. Does the world then return to darkness? How can believers continue to "see"? And what about people who come after Jesus has returned? Is there no possibility of "seeing" for them?

If the meaning of Jesus were identified with theological and/or ethical content, then the church could rely on memory incorporated in its traditions about Jesus. The words about Jesus then could stand in for the Word. Since John refuses to make such an identification, traditions, creeds, even stories (Gospels) do not satisfy. Nothing that belongs to this world, even words about the realm of the Father, can take the place of the realm itself.

This seeming inability of Jesus to be replaced explains the somber mood the disciples show in the discussions with Jesus during that last night before he dies—before he leaves the world. Anyone who has experienced a time when someone important to the very meaning of her life is going away can remember vividly the sadness and anxiety such a departure causes. What will happen to me and my world when this person, who has illumined my darkness, goes away? The very meaning of existence is threatened.

Jesus says at the beginning of the evening, "Where I am going you cannot come" (13:33). Peter then asks, "Where are you going?" (13:36). Later on Jesus expresses the feelings of the group: "Sorrow has filled your hearts" (16:6). "Truly, truly, I say to you, you will weep and lament, but the world will rejoice" (16:20). The disciples do not yet fully understand what Jesus is saying to them. They do hear clearly that he is leaving (deserting?) them.

This mood points to much more than a sense of loss of emotional support. It uncovers a major theological, indeed, christological issue that John must treat in his narrative: the necessity for a continued presence of the light. The enfleshed logos cannot leave the world, even though Jesus must. John solves this dilemma by his brilliant insights into the Christian belief in the Spirit. He radically reworks the meaning held traditionally by believers and even gives the Spirit a new name: the paraclete. In doing this he goes far beyond Paul and begins to move the teaching about the Spirit in a trinitarian direction. It is this reworking which justifies, indeed, necessitates a study of the Spirit in a book on Christology.

The Place of the Paraclete
in the Narrative

Unique among all the Gospels, John indicates that the Spirit comes to the church at the resurrection of Jesus. Jesus breathes on the disciples the Holy Spirit when he appears to them (20:22). Since the Spirit is a reality only to the church, it is appropriate that Jesus' teaching about the Spirit take place not in his encounters with the outside world, but only in the final discourses with the true disciples (the first reference begins at 14:16). Prior to the last night, there are only sporadic appearances of the word *pneuma* and none of *paraklētos*.

Only in chapter 7 is the future bestowal of Spirit on the believers promised, and that in the briefest manner. After Jesus has cited Scripture, "Out of his heart shall flow rivers of living water" (the location of this citation is unknown), the author comments: "Now this he said about the Spirit, which those who believed in him were to receive; for as yet the Spirit had not been given, because Jesus was not yet glorified" (7:39). The reader (who obviously knows about the Spirit as a present reality in the church) learns that the coming of the Spirit is in some way identified with the glorification of Jesus (which he may already sense has something to do with the death-resurrection).

The teaching about the paraclete is enclosed in four discrete blocks of material spaced within a short span of the narrative, beginning at John 14:16 and ending with 16:15. The passages are (1) 14:16–17; (2) 14:25–26; (3) 15:26–27; (4) 16:7–15—only 15 verses in all. That they are such self-contained blocks may suggest that they had an existence as a separate tradition (or even a document) which was taken apart and inserted piece by piece into the discourse as the author of the Gospel saw fit.[1] Each block speaks of the paraclete in different ways. Together they have an importance far beyond their modest length.

The Meaning of the Spirit
in John

If we could only know with assurance what the author meant when he used the term "paraclete" (*paraklētos*)! In other literature the word is used so diversely that scholars cannot be sure about its meaning in the Gospel.[2] In the broadest sense, it seems to mean "helper," which can in more specific contexts be narrowed to "intercessor" or "advocate." A semi-legal sense often shimmers behind the term and its translations, and the possibility that it is a legal metaphor should be kept in mind. Outside of the Gospel the word is used christologically in early texts only in 1 John 2:1. Thus ultimately the Johannine context must determine the translation, rather than the reverse. What is it that each of these sections contributes to the overall meaning of John's theological structure?

1. John 14:16–17 (au. trans.):

> And I will pray the Father, and he will give you another paraclete, to be with you for ever, even the Spirit of truth, whom the world cannot receive, because it neither sees him nor knows him; you know him, for he dwells with you, and will be in you.

The theme of the larger context, 14:1–23, is the eschatological presence of the divine reality within the believer (see chapter 10 below for details). Since the reality of indwelling of the divine in the believer involves the presence of the Spirit, it is absolutely essential that the Spirit be introduced here. As the concluding clause states, "He dwells with you, and will be in you" (14:17).

The beginning of v. 16 startles: The Father "will give you *another* paraclete, to be with you for ever." This implies that there has been already one paraclete; who was [is] it? Almost everyone agrees that it is Jesus who has been the previous paraclete. Jesus as paraclete departs to the Father; the Spirit as paraclete comes to be in the world "for ever."

This gives us our first important hint about the meaning of the Spirit for the author. *The Spirit is an eternal ("for ever") replacement for the enfleshed logos.* Thus it is fair to suggest that all John writes about Jesus is important in interpreting the meaning of "paraclete." Since Jesus functions variously, it is not surprising that no simple definition of the word "paraclete" can suit. Jesus is light, but that leads to judgment as well as life. The legal metaphor emerges as a possibility, but this means that the paraclete is as much "prosecuting attorney" as "defense attorney." In chapter 17 John portrays Jesus as intercessor. Thus since the paraclete is a replacement for everything Jesus is and does, it is perhaps simplest to say that the paraclete comes to reenact in the world the totality of the functions of the enfleshed logos.

2. John 14:25–26 (au. trans.):

> These things I have spoken to you, while I am still with you. But the paraclete, the Holy Spirit, whom the Father will send in my name, he will teach you all things, and bring to your remembrance all that I have said to you.

Here a further important identification is made. Jesus is teacher, and the paraclete is teacher. The Spirit will "teach you all things," yet what "all things" seems to refer to—and indeed is—is "all that I have said to you." Thus the teaching of the paraclete is nothing other, or more, than the teaching of Jesus.

This uncovers a serious historical problem: what John presents as the teaching of Jesus has to be the reflection of years or decades of early Christian thinkers. John surely cannot be so naive as to think that what is said in his Gospel is what was said by the actual, earthly Jesus! Or can he?

A hint has been given to the reader early in the Gospel. In the dialogue with the Jews, after the temple cleansing, Jesus makes a cryptic remark which the Jews do not understand nor, the narrative implies, did the disciples at the time. "When therefore he was raised from the dead, his disciples remembered that he had said this; and they believed the scripture and the word which Jesus had spoken" (2:22).

No, the disciples did not grasp the full import of Jesus while he was alive. Long after his death, the Johannine community believes it has come to a rich and deep understanding of the full meaning of Jesus. But this growing understanding is not a novel, human interpretation. The church has been led by the Spirit to know the significance of Jesus. But since this significance is the real meaning, it is identical with that of the earthly Jesus. Thus the teaching of the paraclete must be identical with Jesus' own teaching. *The Spirit re-presents in the world the reality of the enfleshed logos.* And this in turn means that, ultimately, the teaching of the paraclete makes present the reality of the Father.

3. John 15:26–27 (au. trans.):

> But when the paraclete comes, whom I shall send to you from the Father, even the Spirit of truth, who proceeds from the Father, he will bear witness to me; and you also are witnesses, because you have been with me from the beginning.

Even into one sentence John seems able to pack important new information! We learn here that Jesus himself will send the Spirit, although it proceeds from the Father.

What is important, however, is the introduction of the theme of witnessing. Although we have not dealt with it before, it plays a relatively important role in the Gospel. And here the legal metaphor dominates. In Jewish law the agreement of two witnesses is necessary for proof. This is well known to any reader of the trial narrative of Mark (14:55–59). In John 5:30–47, the question of adequate witnesses for Jesus' claims arises and is answered in various ways. The problem reappears in 8:13–19.

The paraclete is here invoked as one witness for the truth of Jesus. That this passage is playing on the legal metaphor is indicated by the statement that follows: The disciples are the second witness. After the return to the Father, Jesus retains on earth two true witnesses for the continuing earthly trial, that is, the debate between Christianity and the world. The paraclete is true because it re-presents the reality of Jesus himself. The witness of the disciples is true, it is implied, because they have been with Jesus "from the beginning."

But are these really two different witnesses, paraclete and church? Yes and no! Yes, because the church as a collection of finite human individuals is not the divine reality itself. No, because the church is the flesh of the Spirit. Just as the logos has to have flesh to appear in the world, so also the paraclete. His flesh is the church. Thus the witness of the disciples, rightly understood, is the witness of the paraclete.

4. John 16:7–15: This passage, climactic in the series, longest and most involved, is also the most difficult to translate and interpret. It is embedded in a sweeping polyphony, which begins with dark words of threat for the disciples (16:1–2) and ends with the jubilant cry: Be of good cheer, I have conquered the world! (16:33).

Again the context is legal. Proceedings against the believers are predicted (16:1–2): exclusion from synagogues and executions or murders (reflecting the beginning persecution by the Romans?). These predictions are doubtlessly present realities for the community. The believers are not to worry, however, because the paraclete will be among them precisely in these situations. The context may be very close to that pointed to by the Synoptic teaching: "And when they bring you to trial and deliver you up, do not be anxious beforehand what you are to say; but say whatever is given you in that hour, for it is not you who speak, but the Holy Spirit" (Mark 13:11). So in John, when the paraclete comes, he will turn the tables on the accusers, for he will "convict the world" (au. trans.). What this means is now described in a carefully constructed rhetorical passage.

And when he comes, he shall convict (illuminate?) the world
    with regard to sin, vindication, and judgment:
    with regard to sin, in that they do not believe in me;
    with regard to vindication, in that I return to the Father and you see me no
        more;
    with regard to judgment, in that the ruler of this world has been judged.
                                        (John 16:7–11, au. trans.)

The translation problems are substantial, and the interested reader should consult the commentaries. The basic tenor of the passage is clear, however, regardless of decisions about specific words. First of all, the metaphor is without doubt legal. This is the meaning of the ruling verb "to convict." It can also mean "to bring to the light," to "expose." That John intends another of his beloved double-entendres is probably indicated by a somewhat similar passage in chapter 12. There the theme of the glorification of God in the cross of Jesus is sounded, followed by Jesus' affirmation: "Now is the judgment of this world, now shall the ruler of this world be cast out" (John 12:31). To illuminate is both to save and to bring judgment.

All of these convictions by the paraclete are based on the rejection by the world of the enfleshed logos. Sin is refusal to believe in him. Vindication is God's victory over the attempt to extinguish the light by killing Jesus. Judgment, as the reader has already learned (p. 93 below), is the world's own stubborn refusal to come to the light. The "ruler of this world" then stands for the obstinacy of the world itself. The key thing the reader learns is that the paraclete, by continuing the presence of Jesus in the world, continues the function of judgment which the presence of the light inevitably, if unintentionally, causes. As the paraclete re-presents the light, it re-presents the condemnation of the world for its refusal to believe in Jesus Christ.

I am not sure if believers then or now could take much comfort in this definition of the function of the church, for that is what it means. *The act of the paraclete is enfleshed through the act of the church.* The church, if it truly re-presents the saving light from the realm of the Father, is engaged in a gigantic, cosmic trial with the powers of darkness. The church is thus to convict the world, regardless of consequences, if it is to remain true to its calling. Shortly thereafter, the disciples will overhear Jesus say to the Father: "I do not pray that thou shouldst take them out of the world, but that thou shouldst keep them from the evil one" (17:15). There is to be no escape from the responsibility of witness and thus its results. Yet in this very act of witness, which may lead to death, the victory over the world takes place, just as it occurred in the death of the enfleshed logos.

Verses 16:12–15, the final reference to the paraclete, emphasize once again that the words of the paraclete are ultimately the revelation of the Father. "He will guide you into all the truth." Just as Jesus does nothing on his own authority (5:30), so the paraclete speaks only what he hears. And just as Jesus glorifies the Father, so the paraclete will glorify Jesus, "For he will take what is mine and declare it to you"(16:14). But since what is "mine" is that of the Father, the speech of the paraclete is nothing other than the reality of the Father.

Question: How then does the church participate in the victory over the world? Answer: Not in enjoying ease and comfort, not in escaping persecution, even death, but only in remaining true to the witness of the truth, only in allowing its flesh to become the vehicle of the words of the paraclete.

The Implications for Christology

These implications are so clear from what has been said that they can be briefly summarized. The paraclete is actually part of John's Christology, because the Spirit is nothing less or more than the re-presentation of the enfleshed logos in the world. Once the logos has become flesh there is to be no moment in the world's history in which the divine reality does not shine (unless it be the few hours between death and resurrection). Before the resurrected Jesus departs, the Spirit is breathed into the church.

Since the paraclete is the re-presentation of the logos, it replicates in the post-Easter situation every function of logos in the earthly Jesus. The paraclete brings the light of salvation, which is at the same time the light of judgment. The Spirit dwells within believers, enabling them to participate in the divine reality. At the same time the Spirit, through these same believers, reveals the ultimate condemnation on all those who refuse to come to the light. Just as with the enfleshed logos, darkness is hiding from the light—condemnation, the refusal to believe.

John's teaching about the Spirit thus marks a step toward Trinitarian reflections, far beyond anything any other New Testament author presents, even Paul. The Spirit is no longer the transient manifestation of power in some believers. Nor is it the basis of the ethical life, as Paul has it. (John is strangely and disquietingly silent about ethical matters.) And while Paul seems tentatively to move in the direction of the equation of the manifestation of Spirit and the meaning of Christ, John does it in such a grandly self-conscious way that there is hardly any connection between the two theologians at this point.

The Trinitarian direction can be seen in the chain of relationships. The Son reveals the reality of the Father, and the Spirit reveals the reality of the Son. Thus the truth shining through in the life of the church, as it points to the Father-Son in its manifestation and through its witness, is no less a vehicle of the reality of the Father than was Jesus himself. This is the meaning of Jesus' promise to the disciples: "Truly, truly, I say to you, he who believes in me will also do the works that I do; and greater works than these will he do, because I go to the Father" (14:12). The greater works are the eternal re-presentation of the divine reality in all its results, not because the church is a collection of superhuman miracle workers, but because it is the flesh of the paraclete.

CHAPTER TEN

THE WORK OF CHRIST:
BELIEVERS AND UNBELIEVERS

Just as with Paul, John is not playing intellectual games with his Christology. His interpretation has the seriousness of life and death, because this is what he believes are the stakes. Even though in his thought the logos is eternal, the purpose of the eternal Son is the temporal event of being sent by the Father to save the world. As I have tried to argue, the claim of eternality and co-divinity with God is, in fact, a necessary function in John's structure, the purpose of which is to secure the event of salvation. As the prologue (1:1–18) reaches its climax more and more emphasis is placed upon the soteriological act of the logos. And in the narrative itself all attention is placed on the intention and result of the sending of the Son.

Thus, again as with Paul, the Christology cannot be completely understood without incorporating into its structure what Jesus Christ accomplishes in the world and for humanity. John's thought is as radical here as his Christology itself. Indeed, the two go together inseparably. While what we have said so far sets the stage for this final step, to take it requires some careful exegesis of difficult sections of the Gospel, as well as reflection upon complex issues such as mysticism and predestination.

Salvation and Condemnation

John 3:16–21 not only contains the most beloved sentence in the Gospel for many people of faith, it also presents the scholar with one of the thorniest exegetical problems. The passage requires careful analysis.

"For God so loved the world that he gave his only Son, that whoever believes in him should not perish but have eternal life" (v. 16). The purpose of Jesus Christ is to bestow eternal life. That, of course, while beautifully put, is not in and of itself in any way different from the traditional belief of the church. The next verse seems to repeat this thought, but the difference in nuance prepares for the development that is to follow. "For God sent the Son into the world, not to judge [i.e., condemn] the world, but that the world might be saved through him" (v. 17, au. trans.). Why is it explicitly said that the purpose of the sending is not judgment? To emphasize that judgment is not God's intent, even if it is the inevitable result.

"He who believes in him does not come into judgment; but the one not believing has already been judged [i.e., condemned], because he has not believed in the name of the only begotten Son of God" (v. 18, au. trans.). Here new ideas are reached, or are at least stated in novel terms. The believer escapes judgment and hence is saved. Thus believing is salvation. The verbs are this far in the present tense and could be taken literally: salvation is "now," that is, a present event. That this is in fact the intent is clarified by the next clause, in which the ruling tense is the perfect.

In contrast to the believer's not having to stand judgment, the unbelieving person has already been judged. There is no reason to doubt that the eschatological judgment is what is being pointed to; ultimate judgment is a present reality in the midst of this world. According to the text, this judgment is not something forced upon a person, but one which is freely chosen in the act of believing or the act of unbelieving. In fact it could be said that the person does not even know judgment has taken place. All he or she is aware of is that commitment to Christ has been made or has been rejected. It is the purpose of the Gospel to clarify for the person the eschatological meaning of that decision.

The paradoxical contrast between purpose and result of the sending of the Son is repeated in the next sentence. "This is the judgment, that the light has come into the world and people preferred darkness to the light, for their works were evil." (v. 19, au. trans.). Now the paradox is stated in terms of the metaphor of light. The purpose of the light is obviously salvation, but it brings judgment upon those who choose darkness instead of light. The question is, why would anyone prefer darkness to light?

The answer given in the text raises a crucial difficulty: "For their works were evil." The difficulty is compounded by the final sentence of the section. "For everyone doing evil hates the light and does not come to the light, so that his works may not be exposed. But the one doing the truth comes to the light, that his works might be manifested that they have been worked by God" (vv. 20–21, au. trans.).

What is the difficulty? It is that these passages seem to imply that a person is good or evil prior to the potential encounter with the light, and that her goodness or evilness is what determines her willingness or unwillingness to approach. That is, although John elsewhere makes it clear that salvation is dependent upon "believing in," here "believing in" is itself dependent upon something prior, namely good deeds, and we seem to be in a theology of "works-righteousness" that sits poorly with John's basic affirmations.[1]

How to deal with this apparent contradiction? If we start, as we must, with the judgment that salvation in John is tied solely with believing in the light, then there are two possibilities. One is to relegate these sentences to a source foreign to the original author, perhaps the editor who many believe is responsible for the Gospel as it presently stands. The other is to interpret the questionable sentences so that they agree with the rest of John. At this point many commentators appeal to Rudolf Bultmann who has most heroically attempted to bring them into line with the Gospel as a whole. I can do no better. According to Bultmann, it is not that prior to encounter with the light some people are good and others bad. Rather, "Before the encounter with the Revealer the life of all people moves in darkness, in sin." What happens in the encounter is that a person is challenged to decide for or against his past as he decides for his future, "so that in this decision for the first time his past is given its meaning, that is, by refusing to believe he makes definitive the validity of its worldly-sinful character, or by believing he destroys this worldly-sinful character."[2]

What Bultmann is saying is that the decision of a person about the light is in effect a decision about his past, whether or not he affirms or rejects his past worldly life and its values. To come to the light thus means to loose oneself from the world of darkness and to accept judgment upon it and one's prior participation in it. This is, it seems to me, a profound statement of what John's thought could be, and perhaps should be. Whether it is fair to the syntax of the sentences is less clear to me. In any case, to use these verses to conclude that salvation in John is dependent upon works would be surely false.

Summary. The light appears in the world with the intent to draw all people to it and thus to save the world. What results, however, is a deep split within human society. Some are drawn to the light and accept their life from it. By doing this they have already entered the realm of salvation. Others reject the light, preferring to remain in the world of darkness, which, tragically, they do not understand to be darkness at all. This remaining in darkness while still alive in this world is condemnation. The presence of the light in the world effects eschatological salvation and condemnation. There is no need or even a place for a future judgment, certainly not one based on works.

Present Eschatology

To this kind of thought scholars have given the name "present" or "realized eschatology." While prominent at seminal places in earliest Christianity—notably in Jesus and Paul as well as in the Gospel of John—it is so alien to traditional church teaching that it is hard for one encountering it for the first time to grasp. We have already seen it prominently displayed in Paul, although for the apostle the final act is still future; yet in John it is so persistently pursued that it reaches a clarity which confronts the reader in a way she cannot escape. For John it is fair to conclude: if salvation does not begin now (in this life), then it never begins. The full import of such a claim must await further explanation in the narrative.

After the initial statement in 3:16–21, the author is content to let out hints here and there, until the final discourses of Jesus with the disciples. In the dialogue with the Samaritan woman the issue of the location of worship appears. Where does one truly worship—at the Temple of Jerusalem or on the Samaritan mountain? Jesus cuts through that issue with the Johannine answer, "But the hour is coming, *and now is,* when the true worshipers will worship the Father in spirit and truth" (4:23). Since for John "the hour" is the eschatological hour, he is proclaiming the presence of the ultimate reality in which believers have direct access to God. What this really means must again await explanation in the final discourse.

In chapter 5, where the theme in part is eschatological judgment and life, Jesus says: "Truly, truly, I say to you, the hour is coming, *and now is,* when the dead will hear the voice of the Son of God, and those who hear will live" (5:25). The radical "presentizing" of the notion of resurrection obviously startled copyists and caused a number of variations in some manuscripts (including a removal of the key phrase, "and now is"). The thought of John is, however, clear. Resurrection begins now in the faithful hearing of the Son. Eternal life is a present possibility for all who believe.[3]

The dialogue with Martha in the Lazarus story provides another opportunity for the author to strike a glancing blow for a present eschatology. Martha confesses: "I know that he [Lazarus] will rise again in the resurrection at the last day" (11:24). Jesus implicitly corrects her futuristic eschatology. "I am the resurrection and the life; he who believes in me, though he die, yet shall he live, and whoever lives and believes in me shall never die" (11:25). The idea of life after death is, of course, affirmed; what is different is the last statement. The act of "believing in" is the beginning of eternal life itself.

Finally, Jesus utters what comes the closest to a definition of eternal life in his prayer to the Father in chapter 17. "And this is eternal life, that they know thee the only true God, and Jesus Christ whom thou hast sent" (17:3). Eternal life is knowing the divine reality.

By now this should not really surprise. We have sensed that "believing in" and "knowing" are similar, if not identical acts of commitment. We have known since chapter 3 that believing is salvation. We can even attempt our own definition with the information at hand. Salvation is the quality of existence in which one apprehends the divine reality through the act of

committed knowing. This is not quite right. What is at issue is a perspec-
tive/perception based on commitment to the divine reality made known
through the enfleshed logos. That is, eternal life is perception of self/world
determined by awareness of the divine reality.

Even this does not say everything. Its strength is that it describes something real to human experience. One's apprehension of all reality is radically different because of this committed knowing. Yet it sounds—indeed
is—too subjective. Is this quality of being anything more than an act of my
psyche? And further, in what way can one call it eternal?

To see how John deals with these questions, however he may himself
have framed them, we need to look at a most important text, analysis of
which I have postponed until now.

Eternal Life as Participation
in Divine Reality

The text is 14:1–23, which begins with a statement many readers will
remember from the KJV: "In my Father's house are many mansions."(v.
2). The path to the conclusion of the section, in which the Johannine meaning is finally disclosed, is tortuous. I must ask patience from the reader,
especially since the interpretation may startle, and perhaps disturb many.

The larger setting is Book II (see chap. 7, under "The Plot of the
Gospel," above), the final discourse of Jesus with his disciples. John uses
this section to teach about the purpose of the church and to reveal some
of the deep meanings hinted at in Jesus' dialogue with outsiders in Book
I. The correct interpretation of eternal life is an obvious must, and the
author turns to this theme in chapter 14. On the way to revealing his understanding he has to correct traditional Jewish and Christian views, views
which one can, for example, find readily in the other Gospels.

The section is artfully constructed as a dialogue between Jesus and the
disciples. Yet the role of the latter is restricted to the raising of questions
at key points in Jesus' teaching. The questions arise when Jesus is suggesting a perspective different from that of the usual Jewish-Christian future-
oriented eschatology. They always imply that usual point of view, and they
function in the dialogue to provide Jesus the opportunity to correct or
change that view. A reader familiar with Greek philosophical or literary
dialogues will recognize this device.

The RSV changes "mansion" to the very inelegant "room"; this is an
accurate translation for our day (in Elizabethan English "mansion" did not
carry the connotation of luxurious surroundings). The Greek word, *monē,*
is also very commonplace and unspecific. It simply means a dwelling
place, a house, or a room to stay in. The correlate verb, *menein,* is again

very ordinary and nonspecific, meaning "to stay," "lodge," "remain," "abide." The question the reader must keep in mind throughout the discussion is where these rooms really are.

The dialogue begins with Jesus promising what would be interpreted in the usual view as a blessed life in heaven (vv. 2–3). Jesus is going (to heaven) to prepare a place for believers, will come again (the "second coming" at the Parousia), and will take them to himself (understood as in heaven), so that Jesus and believers will be reunited in an eternal life in heaven. But then he adds, "And you know the way where I am going" (v. 4). This would probably be taken to refer to the various apocalyptic "maps" which described the way through the heavenly spheres to God. Sometimes these maps, which were based on a "geographical" understanding of the way, could be very complicated.

At this point the first questioner (Thomas) interjects: "Lord, we do not know where you are going; how can we know the way?" (v. 5). Jesus has not provided the expected "map." He responds with an epiphany statement: "I am the way, and the truth, and the life; no one comes to the Father, but by me" (v. 6). With this Jesus says something as yet incomprehensible. He is the map (the way). Since the aim of the seeker of eternal life was the vision of God (to be enjoyed, of course, in heaven), Jesus presents himself as the way to the Father. And then he implies that knowing him is the same thing as knowing the Father. "Henceforth you know him and have seen him" (v. 7).

The goal of the heavenly journey, normally "located" at the end of time, is now a present possibility in the presence of Jesus! Not surprisingly this is too bold a reinterpretation for the disciples to grasp immediately. Hence a second questioner (Philip) rises to the debate: "Lord, show us the Father and we shall be satisfied" (v. 8). Jesus now makes explicit the implication of his previous statement—"He who has seen me has seen the Father" (v. 9)—and adds the first of what I will call "indwelling statements." "Do you not believe that I am in the Father and the Father in me?" (v. 10). This gives the ground for seeing the Father in Jesus: their divine realities are mutually indwelling. The indwelling language is repeated in the following verse for emphasis.

A few sentences later appears the first paraclete pericope (vv. 16–17), which we have already analyzed.[4] The reason it has to appear at this point in the dialogue is clear from the last clause in the pericope: "You know him [the paraclete], for he dwells with you, and will be in you" (v. 17). Another "indwelling" statement, this time linking Spirit with believer. It is crucial to note that the word "dwell" is *menein*, the verb correlate to the noun *monē*, "room," with which the whole dialogue began. The reader is thus alerted that there may be some relationship between the rooms promised the believers, seemingly at the eschaton in heaven, and the dwelling of the Spirit in the believer in this life. This relationship will be clarified as the indwelling language intensifies. So far, the Father and Son are said to be indwelling, and the paraclete and believer. The decisive connection between Father and believer has not yet been made.

Jesus then promises: "I will not leave you desolate; I will come to you. Yet a little while, and the world will see me no more, but you will see me"(vv. 18–19). The first part of the statement is readily understandable in terms of the traditional eschatology. But when Jesus adds that "the world will see me no more," it implicitly contradicts that tradition, in which the event of the Parousia of Christ is to be cosmically visible. In fact a "Q" statement makes that explicit. "For as the lightning comes from the east and shines as far as the west, so will be the coming of the Son of man" (Matt. 24:27). By his statement in John's dialogue, Jesus denies this cosmic dimension of the eschaton.

The inevitable question is postponed, however, until Jesus makes the needed connection in the indwelling sequence. "In that day you will know that I am in my Father, and you in me, and I in you" (v. 20). Now the mutual indwelling of Father/Son incorporates the believer, doubtlessly because of the paraclete's indwelling with the believer, although that part of the chain is not mentioned here. *This is the decisive affirmation of eschatological reality.* To believe in Jesus means participation in divine reality. And since the indwelling Spirit channels this divine reality, future believers can participate in the Father equally as well as the disciples who were in the presence of the enfleshed logos.

Jesus then continues: "He who loves me will be loved by my Father, and I will love him and manifest myself to him" (v. 21). The quality of the indwelling as love is introduced here, but the next questioner will pick up on the final clause, "manifest myself to him." "Judas (not Iscariot) said to him, 'Lord, how is it that you will manifest yourself to us, and not to the world?' " (v. 22). The alert Judas has heard two contradictory statements from Jesus, contradictory at least to the traditional view. The eschatological Parousia will occur only to believers; it will not be the expected cataclysmic, cosmic event! How, Judas asks, are we to think this possible?

With this question the denouement of the dialogue is prepared for and occurs in the next statement by Jesus. "If a person loves me, he will keep my word, and my Father will love him, and *we will come to him and make our home (monē) with him*"(v. 23). The home promised at the beginning of the chapter is finally revealed to be the believer indwelled by the divine reality. It is not a geographical place in heaven at the end of time. *It is the*

*believer who participates now, in this time and place, within the world, in
the divine realm of the Father.*

This is the objective ground for the subjective apprehension with which
we began. Eternal life is a new perception, thus a new subjective reality.
But this is grounded in the divine act of indwelling. Indeed, this objective
basis makes the word "eternal" meaningful.

Here is the most radical statement of present eschatology in the New
Testament. All of the previous statements and hints given in the Gospel find
their full meaning here. Not only does participation in the realm of the
Father begin in this life, this is its only beginning. There is to be no future
cataclysmic event. Nothing is said about the end or destruction of the
world. Nor is anything really said about life after death, although it is clear
that the phrase "eternal life" means just that: the participation in the divine
reality that begins in this life will continue forever.

The author wishes the reader to focus attention solely on the situation
in this world, in this time. There is to be no escape into fantasy about what
it will be like some day. In fact John blocks all escape from the cold realities of this world. Eternal life is lived within a world which really believes
that killing Christians is a divine duty (16:2). "I do not pray that thou
shouldst take them out of the world, but that thou shouldst keep them from
the evil one" (17:15). No "stop the world, I want to get off" for John's
church! Just as Jesus came as light in the darkness, so must the church
through the paraclete continue that shining in the midst of darkness, hostility, opposition. And yet in this present the believer participates in the
divine reality and, indeed, re-presents that reality to the world.

Mysticism in the Gospel?

The question can no longer be avoided: Is John's picture of the relation
between the divine reality and the believer one that can be called mysticism? This has long been debated; the way I have described John's Christology certainly opens the possibility for a positive answer. Of course the
question itself depends upon an even more difficult prior issue: what do
we mean by "mysticism"?

Risking great oversimplification, I suggest that the many definitions fall
into two major categories. The first is *affective:* the mystic has overwhelm-
ing experiences of the divine. The second is *ontological:* the mystic
becomes or is unified with the divine. The first need not concern us here.
John seems to have little interest in the affective life, even if he does depict
Jesus expressing emotion on occasion. What experiential dimensions the
indwelling may have are not even hinted at.

The ontological is a possibility, however, given the emphasis on indwelling. I have carefully used the word "participation" to describe the mutual indwelling of believer with the divine reality. Would it be accurate to go further, to speak of the "unification" of the human with the divine? In John's scheme does the person become divine in the indwelling?

The terminology is dangerous, because the entire mainline Judeo-Christian tradition has fought vigorously against the incursion of ontological mysticism into its theology. Basic views of monotheism and the separation of God and person seem violated by such mysticism. Consider the suspicion medieval theologians had toward Meister Eckhart and the attitude of the rabbis to the cabala. Since John is in the canon and is thus by definition "orthodox," there is naturally great reluctance to entertain seriously the possibility that John does present an ontological mysticism. Bultmann, for example, with his existential (decisional) Protestant stance, soundly rejected the possibility.[5]

If we are to be honest in our exegesis, however, such a strong inclination from a theological perspective must not overrule what we find in the text. In my judgment, the definition of eternal life as mutual indwelling of the human with the divine makes it necessary to raise the question afresh. Yet these very exegetical considerations should make one cautious about a simple answer either yes or no.

In the first place it is clear that John thinks in categories of act and will, when thinking of the divine reality, not in terms of being or substance. He cannot, therefore, have conceived of indwelling in terms of substantial identity. The believer does not become "by nature" one with God.

Second, whatever meaning we ultimately ascribe to the indwelling, it is an event which for the believer happens in time and as a result of the act of "believing in." The indwelling is not an eternal reality, due to the identity of nature, but one which comes to be in the historical process due to God's act and the human decision. In effect the Gnostic view of the self as a spark of the divine is rejected. The believer's life is eternal in the sense that now once begun it may continue forever, not that it reached back for all eternity. At this point John is at one with most of early Christianity.

Third, even eternal life is not assured simply by a one-time decision. In a passage we have not yet looked at (15:1–11), John makes clear the necessity of continued faithfulness. The metaphor is taken from viniculture. Jesus is the vine; believers, the branches. The Father is the vinedresser. "Every branch of mine that bears no fruit, he takes away, and every branch that does bear fruit he prunes, that it may bear more fruit" (15:2). "If anyone does not dwell in me, he is cast forth as a branch and withers" (15:6, au. trans.).

The thought gets complicated here. By "believing in" a person is granted eternal life, and yet that life ceases to be eternal if continued "believing in" does not occur. Eternal life, and this means the indwelling as well, is dependent upon decisional faithfulness. The reason why Bultmann interprets the "mystical" passages in the light of the decision of faith is easy to understand.

Thus "ontological mysticism" is probably an inappropriate description of John's thought. The indwelling, while "eternal," is nevertheless a historical event, or better, a sequence of historical events—the continued necessity to believe and to bear fruit. Perhaps the term "mysticism" itself should be avoided and we remain content with the more ambiguous but more pliable term "participation."[6] In the indwelling, participation in divine reality takes place, and this participation is eternal life. Ultimately what names we use are not important. The text can be permitted to have the final word (14:8–9).

> Philip: "Show us the Father, and we shall be satisfied."
> Jesus: "He who has seen me has seen the Father."

Predestination in the Gospel?

A second question, equally puzzling, concerns whether there is predestinarian thought in the Gospel. The texts we have studied thus far have implied, it is fair to say, that persons have freedom of decision. Whether or not they come to the light, whether or not they believe, is something they decide for themselves (e.g., 3:18–21). The coming of the divine reality to indwell in the self is dependent upon the intentionality of the individual ("If a person loves me, he will keep my word . . . and we will come to him and make our home with him'—14:23, au. trans.). Even the remaining in this relationship is dependent upon continued "believing in" on the part of the person: "If anyone does not dwell in me, he is cast forth as a branch and withers" (15:6, au. trans.).

But there are other texts which imply the contrary: only those whom God *has already chosen* come to and remain in faith. While such texts are scattered throughout the narrative, it is only in chapter 17 that they become so concentrated that the issue seems to be decided.[7] Jesus has power "to give eternal life to all whom thou [God] hast given him" (v. 2). This statement, that the believers have been given to the enfleshed logos by a decision of the Father, is then repeated in vv. 6, 9, and 24. This is sufficient for Barrett to conclude: "Prominence is given in this chapter to the idea of predestination."[8]

That texts can be marshaled on both sides certainly suggests that John himself made no final decision that resolves the tension. Both positions are allowed to stand, doubtlessly because both make sense to his experience. That persons come to faith by their own decision is a seemingly obvious fact of universal experience. It is *I* who decided! And yet that one may be led, that there is an element of surprise within the volitional consciousness of the self is also a datum of experience. Bultmann expresses this dimension clearly.

> Admittedly, it [the decision] is wrought by God, but not as if the working of God took place before faith, or, so to speak, behind it; rather, God's working takes place exactly in it. For when the Revelation encounters faith, the reply which faith makes to the Revelation's question feels itself to have been wrought by the question itself. In making its decision, faith understands itself as a gift.[9]

A third experiential dimension is probably at work here. John's stance toward the outside world shows certain signs of defensiveness.[10] Some have believed, but apparently not many, and the burning question is Why? Why have so many refused to come to the light? Some Gnostics could answer this question by claiming that only a few were spiritual by nature and were thus capable of receiving truth. John cannot go this route; perhaps his tendency to see an ultimate divine decision behind the historical decisions is his way of dealing with the issue. Commenting on John 17:6 Ernst Haenchen writes:

> The riddle of predestination is never mentioned by name in the Gospel of John. The Evangelist would not have known it from any sort of tradition, but from bitter experience with those over whom the word had been poured without leaving a trace, the word that illuminated the whole of life for him.[11]

However we may decide such matters for ourselves in our own theology, it is best to allow the Gospel to remain in its fecund ambiguity. The richness of John's own reflection keeps him from an ideological commitment to either side. About one thing John is sure. The gracious act of the Father in sending the Son is prior to, and thus provides the only ground for, the decision of faith.

PART 3

CONCLUSION

CHAPTER ELEVEN

TRUE GOD AND TRUE WORLD: VISION AND REALITY

To encounter and face up to the Christologies of Paul and John is to wrestle with two angels! Like Jacob, we know we have been in a fight. But even if we are exhausted, we should also acknowledge amazement at both the grandeur and subtlety of the two premier theologians of early Christianity. The vistas of cosmic proportions and the insights into one's inward being join in both christological structures to give us a vision of a new self in a new world.

The Relationship between Paul and John

The question inevitably arises, indeed has intrigued researchers for a long time, what relationships might exist between these giants. From a historical perspective, of course, the question can only be what John may have learned from Paul. Did the author of the Gospel know the Pauline letters, or some of them? Was Paul's theology so "in the air" in John's background that he knew the general drift of Paul's Christology, whether or not he had read the letters?

The answer to these questions, insofar as they concern the issue of a historical connection between John and Paul, has to be no. The previous chapters lead us to a negative conclusion: no significant relationship exists between the letters and the Gospel in at least three important respects.

First, the vocabulary is different. Given the obvious fact that both authors have emerged from previous Christian tradition, there is bound to be some overlap. The title "Son of God," for example, occurs in both. The verb "to believe" occurs in both. These self-explanatory similarities are overshadowed, however, by the differences. The great Pauline words "justification" and "grace" are virtually absent from John. Certainly they play no role in the basic structure of the Gospel. "Son of man" and "the Son," on the other hand, so important to John, are entirely absent (in the case of "Son of man") or virtually so (in the case of the absolute use of "the Son") in Paul. One can summarize: what is important to Paul, John ignores; and what is important to John was not learned from Paul.

Second, the christological structure is different. Paul's building blocks come from the legal system and out of these he builds a structure that is a giant legal metaphor. Emphasis is on the different worlds created by opposing understandings of the judge and the rules by which the persons standing before the judge's bench discover their fate. In this structure the concepts of grace and justification have essential roles to play. Faith is essentially that quality of existence made possible by the new understanding of the judge.

While there is a juridical flavor to much of John's theology, the basic structure is entirely different from the apostle's. The two worlds, the realm of the Father in contrast to that of this world, the descending/ascending Son of man as the connection between the two realms—all this is John's basic view upon which he builds his interpretation of Jesus as the revelation in this world of the divine reality. It is certainly the case that Paul knows of the preexistent Christ, but in his system it does not function in a crucial way. John, on the other hand, is absolutely dependent on the preexistence of Christ for his structure to work.

A third argument for the basic independence of the two systems is based on the location of Paul and John in the trajectories of tradition. Here we can appeal to evidence outside of the principal documents themselves. Paul seems to have belonged to the mainstream Hellenistic church. He functioned and developed his own theological position in dialogue with this basic tradition. In the Pauline trajectory, the several deutero-Pauline writings show how thinkers took Paul and developed him to fit their own situations. These writings show little affinity with Johannine structures, even if preexistence and cosmological motifs are strong in Colossians and Ephesians.

On the Johannine side, scholars are basically in agreement that the Gospel is the fruit of a school or community in which the basic Johannine structure, motifs, and style were developed over a period of years. To find antecedents to the Gospel itself, therefore, one must look to the developments in this community which, at some point prior to the Gospel itself, had already moved toward its distinctive mode of thinking. And while it is true that the Johannine epistles, later documents of this school, are perhaps closer to the Pauline perspective, that is due to their general movement back toward mainstream Hellenistic Christianity, not indicative of a renewal of Pauline emphases perhaps submerged by the Gospel.

All of these considerations make it certain that there can have been no historical connection between John and anything that would count as the distinctive Pauline theology. If there was such a connection, then the Johannine community and the author of the Gospel have so completely restructured and relanguaged Paul that he is unrecognizable. It is simplest to conclude that John developed his own position in an intellectual environment that had not been touched by the Pauline documents.

This lack of a historical connection makes it all the more remarkable that *in substance there is a profound relationship.* The content of a theology does not lie ultimately in its language, concepts, and structure, but rather in that relationship between persons and God to which the intellectual expressions point. Thus the radical difference at the level of expression between Paul and John does not say, in and of itself, anything about the possible similarity of the deep meaning behind the expressions.

In this book I have tried to point to this deep level of meaning in the two structures, using the language each author had chosen as his vehicle. Now I want to suggest what seem to me to be some profound similarities of understanding about what really is at issue between persons and the God revealed in Jesus Christ.

Visions of Worlds

Creation

Both Paul and John affirm that God, the Father of Jesus Christ, created the cosmos. In the light of two thousand years of Christian thought, this seems axiomatic, a truism. But for someone who took the distortion of the world (sin) as seriously as did our authors, this axiom could have been called in question. Marcion and other Gnostics either explicitly or in effect denied the identity of creator with savior God. In the face of a serious, tragic view of this world, to affirm that the savior God created it took courage and a complex thought structure. Marcion's view is easier if more simplistic.

Paul, it is to be granted, tends to assume rather than explicitly affirm the theology of creation, but it is certainly presupposed in all he says. John, on the other hand, heroically refuses to give up on the claim, even though it complicates his dualism. An explicit statement appears only in the prologue, but many other themes he uses assume such an identity between creator and redeemer.

What this means is that in "salvation" creation is not trashed, discarded, annihilated. Salvation means a restoration, a return of world to its rightful order in relation to God. But this is to jump ahead.

The Vision of the Fallen World

If God is indeed creator of the world, why is not all right with it? How do we even come to believe there is something wrong? Of course, there is the obvious brutality, hatred, and callousness. But by and large, civilized folk live in an ordered, functioning, moral world and need to view the brutality only as aberration of created order, not as symptom of a universal distortion. There is no evidence, either, that our authors lived in a historical situation where civilized order was threatened by excessive brutality.

Yet Paul and John agree, however different is their language, that humanity is sick to its heart. This sickness is not only, or even primarily, manifested in acts of violence but is to these seers made visible in all of society, even in its moral seriousness. Paul and John can sense it in the most pious of acts and persons. The apostle finds it in earnest ethical strivings (Romans 7); the evangelist believes that behind the intent to kill believers lies an ostensible religious act of devotion (16:2). Paul claims that the characteristic of this world is the attempt to justify oneself by one's own deeds. John says simply that it is the world over which darkness reigns. But they are at one in the conviction that this sickness is pervasive, universal.

They are also at one in insight about the cause of this distortion. *Humans are sick because they do not know who their creator really is.* They may know the name; they may call upon the divine; they may earnestly attempt to live out of the divine will. But, tragically, the god upon whom they call is not God at all, but a false image created in the anxiety of human fear.

Paul sees the distortion caused because humans are afraid to believe in a God who gives life. If life is to be secured, humans must make their own way, must find a way to create their own salvation, must justify themselves by their works. Thus the God who truly is, the God who gives life, must be repressed and imprisoned and falsified. The God who justifies by grace cannot be permitted to rise to consciousness. If she does, then the entire program of self-justification, upon which all civilization is based, will be threatened. To permit the true God to arise would manifest the falseness of the world humans have created. Thus the true God is "exchanged" for an image of a god who rewards human attempts to justify themselves. The cause of the distorted world is ignorance of the true God, but, as I have suggested, for Paul this is willful ignorance. Human society wills not to know. It is a societal conspiracy.

John is in agreement with Paul. The cause of distorted human civilization is willful ignorance. The true God is not known; indeed people refuse to know him. John gives us no story of the "fall," or even an analysis such as Paul does in Romans 1. He simply says that the created world has become dark. That this darkness is volitional, however, is seen in the refusal of people to come to the light when it shines in the world (John 1:11; 3:16–21). Salvation is to know the true God (17:3), but it is obvious that for John most people refuse to come to this knowledge.

What, then, do people in their ignorance create in place of the transcend-

ent God? At this point John is not as explicit as Paul, but there are implications. If the transcendent is not acknowledged, not "known," then God
must be created from the immanent, from the realm of this world. Religion
and its symbolizations, intended to point toward the transcendent, become
the divine itself. The symbols become reified and thus are no longer symbols. Paul Tillich's language is pertinent. One's ultimate concern is falsely
attached to that which is not truly ultimate.

The final tragedy is that the ignorant world does not know one crucial
thing: that it is ignorant about the reality of God. Both Paul and John agree
here. What they set themselves against is not blatant brutality but a world
enamored of its own piety and moral seriousness. Indeed, it is precisely
the religious person who is most blinded—by the very fact that he is religious. It is the religious person who thinks her world full of truth, goodness, and beauty.

Paul can say of unbelieving Israel that it has zeal for God, but the zeal
is not based on knowledge; it is ignorant of the righteousness of God—thus
is ignorant of the true God. John, in an insightful passage, shows he is also
aware of the blindness. At the conclusion of the healing of the blind man
in chapter 9, Jesus proclaims: "For judgment I came into this world, that
those not seeing may see and those seeing may become blind" (9:39). The
Pharisees ask a rhetorical question: "Surely we are not blind?" Jesus
responds: "If you were blind, you would not have sin; but now you say,
'We see.' Your sin remains" (9:40-41, au. trans.). Here the Pharisees are
judged precisely because they claim sight when, from Jesus' perspective,
they live in blindness. The tragedy is that they do not know they are blind.

The false world created by humans who have separated themselves from
the true God is thus a closed system. That is, there is nothing within the
system which can point to its falseness. Not everyone within it is content,
finds happiness, functions successfully. Nevertheless evaluations on one's
place within the system are given by the system itself. From the standpoint
of the system, if something is wrong, it is not the system but the failure
of the individual or group to function within it. Only something from outside the system can call the system itself into question. Only something
from outside can condemn the world as false and reveal the possibilities
for a new world.

Jesus Christ as Revealer

Jesus Christ breaks into this closed system, discloses its falseness, its
alienation from the true God, by revealing who the true God is and thus
making possible a new world in true obedience to the true God. At the
deepest level this is how both Paul and John have experienced the sending

of the Son. While their ways of expressing this depth experience differ considerably, I believe both are pointing to this shattering revelation of God to a self-enclosed world when they speak about Jesus Christ. In both language systems Jesus Christ functions to make the divine reality known to people who have been cut off by their world from this ultimate truth.

We have described both Christologies from this perspective in previous chapters. Here it is only necessary to summarize. Paul knows that the world interprets God falsely as one who justifies by works, by one's deeds, by one's own aggressive construction of self and world. The true God revealed in Christ, on the contrary, is the God who lovingly and freely graces persons with the gift of life. True, authentic life is sheer gift. Paul perceives this revelation primarily in the cross and resurrection of Jesus Christ, a revelation which points back to the very reality of the self-giving God. Responding in faith, those who commit themselves to this God live in a new world of genuine freedom, joy, peace, and love.

The Gospel of John portrays an enfleshed logos who discloses to people the realm of the Father. "He who has seen me has seen the Father." While the entire incarnation is to be "seen" as an act of divine love, the most insight-full moment is the self-giving in Jesus' death. Through his own quite different language system, John shows that he sees the significance of the cross in much the same way as Paul.

Our authors agree at yet another essential point. For neither thinker is the true God revealed through theological or ethical teachings *of* or *about* Jesus. Propositional statements, whether in Scripture or creeds, may point to the reality; they are not the reality themselves. Paul, of course, proclaims what God has done in Christ but for this does not rely on any tradition of the teaching of the earthly Jesus. The fact that faith is essential for salvation shows that Paul knows proclamation without experiential appropriation is not sufficient.

While John writes a Gospel, in it Jesus reveals only that he is the revealer. The reader sees the realm of the Father by "seeing" Jesus. I would suggest that neither Paul nor John would find any collection of the teaching of Jesus or any creed about Jesus adequate to communicate his understanding of Christology. These can be part of the building blocks of the structure. But unless the structure succeeds in pointing beyond itself to the divine reality itself, it becomes reified and thus part of this world from which grip the apostle and the evangelist are trying to free us.

Christology as Theo-logy

It should now be clear that for our authors the person and work of Jesus Christ is the absolute center of their reflections. Paul and John are thus a sharp rebuttal and embarrassment to modern liberal Christian attempts to do an end-around of Christology in theological constructions. This is so because for those who would remain content with some vague teaching about God, the question immediately becomes: but how do you know God? For Paul and John the answer can only be: through Jesus Christ. Without Christ-ology there can be no Christian theo-logy (in the sense of an understanding of the reality of God). And yet, if the function of Jesus Christ is to reveal God, then the ultimate aim of a Christ-ology is to point beyond itself—to enable one to speak of God. Christ-ology makes a specifically Christian theo-logy possible.

Christology is central; yet it points beyond itself. The dynamic of the thought of both Paul and John suggests this paradox. Christology ultimately means a redefinition of God, and if reflection on Jesus Christ loses this purpose, it will not remain true to the insights of our authors. In this sense the subordination found in Paul in 1 Cor. 15:27–28 reflects the functional dynamic of his Christology. That God may be "all in all" (1 Cor. 15:28, au. trans.) is the final aim of all Paul has to say.[1]

Is there an implication in this paradox for conversation between Christians and others? I think so, if we reflect carefully. On the one hand, the Christian, just as Paul and John, has experienced God through Jesus Christ, and thus cannot speak about God without speaking about Jesus Christ. This insistence on the necessity of Christology remains the "scandal of particularity" in ecumenical theological discussions and has to be accepted as absolutely necessary.

On the other hand, since the ultimate purpose of speaking about Jesus Christ is to speak about God, the Christian can and should make clear that Christology always points beyond itself. That for Christians Jesus Christ is the vehicle, the mediator, of the experience of God, does not mean Jesus Christ is the only mediator for everyone. To know the only true God is the goal; the avenues to that goal may not exclusively be the rights of Christians. This in no way calls into question the validity of the revelation of God through Jesus Christ. It simply leaves open the possibility that God breaks into the world in ways other than that experienced by those who call upon the name of Jesus.

This openness is not foreign to the intent of either Paul or John. Is it not remarkable that in Romans, when Paul wants to highlight an example of the person who has faith, and therefore is in true relation to the true God, he does not bring forth a believer in Jesus but Abraham who has not known Jesus! And if we have correctly drawn the implications from John's Christology, then the naming of the revealer of God always belongs to the immanent world and is not part of the transcendent reality itself. Naming is secondary to participation in that reality. That others may use names different from the ones Christians choose does not in and of itself invalidate the authenticity of the revealer pointed to by those different names. Even the highly exclusive-sounding claim, "No one comes to the Father, but by me" (John 14:6), must be interpreted in this context. It does not mean that no one comes to the Father save those who have the correct names, but rather that no one can participate in God apart from a mediator who is himself participatory in the divine reality. The naming is secondary. And how does one know? "Come and see!"

Thus the centrality of Jesus Christ in the thinking of Paul and John is misinterpreted if it is taken to mean a parochialism or a narrow exclusivism based on theology used as a reified ideology. Only through christological thinking can Christians be responsive and responsible to the larger ecumenical struggles better to understand God and the world.

The Realization of the Vision

Paul and the author of the Gospel of John agree in one final, perhaps most important point of all. The vision described in their Christology is not simply utopian fantasizing. For them the vision has become a reality in the midst of the world of sin and death, a reality for all those who appropriate the vision, all those who "believe in." This is the meaning of realized eschatology, that eternal life is a possibility now and can be experienced in our own apparently finite time and space.

The emphasis by Paul and John upon present realization has been sufficiently described above to need no repetition here. The question, however, still haunts us: is this mere intellectualization or is it actually experiential? That they claim it to be experiential does not in itself prove anything. Obviously we cannot document through the texts what was the actual experiential reality either of themselves or of their communities.

Nonetheless, we can take confidence in their insistence that what they are talking about is not to be equated with the words they use. The words point beyond themselves to the reality of the true God and the person who has faith, who "believes in." Would someone indulging merely in intellectual fantasy make such a clear distinction? I do not believe so. If they are so certain that behind the words lies the reality they are using words to describe, they must themselves have been in touch with that reality and have believed that that reality was available for their communities as well. Paul must have known the freedom, joy, peace, and love he writes about. John must have experienced the participation in the divine reality through the paraclete, even if he chose not to write about it. Perhaps he did not think it possible. Even so, the ultimate challenge is not to rely upon the authority even of these theological giants, but to "come and see!"

Another question haunts us: How did they come to know the presence of the divine reality? Neither of them knew Jesus according to the flesh. Was it through individual, inspired encounter with the resurrected Christ mediated through their inward psyche? They certainly write intensely about the presence and power of the Spirit. Was it channeled through life in the communities, through the sharing of peace, joy, and love? Paul expressly says how important his churches were for his own sustenance, and the reconstruction of the history of the Johannine communities shows that John is not an isolated giant, but a reflector of the experience of the groups in which he was nurtured. There is no surer mediator of personal formation than a community which shares a distinctive experience.

Was it through hearing others proclaim the act of God in Jesus Christ? We have stressed that words are a reflection on experience; it is equally true that words, when they are living witnesses to experience, are themselves powerful transformers and communicators of experience.

None of these possibilities are mutually exclusive, and indeed they must overlap in concrete situations. And while they are inevitably indirect communications of the act of God in Christ, these socio-psychological manifestations were understood by Paul and John to be authentic encounters with the divine reality itself. Scientifically their claim cannot be denied as a possibility; theologically it can be affirmed. Only through experiences which can be described in socio-psychological terms can encounters with the divine reality occur.

Ultimately, I would conclude, the Christologies of Paul and John leave us with the challenge (and threat!) that to encounter the words in which these Christologies are encased may upset and change us and the world in which we have lived. They may precipitate a scary crisis which jolts us out of our familiar, if dreary reality, into a new world of light and joy. They may mediate afresh to us the God who is and has always been at hand to relate to us in love and grace.

We have the same avenues as did Paul and John to experience God's act in Christ. But actually we have at least one advantage over them. We have their own words, an exciting and profound way through which the God in Jesus Christ can be revealed to us. Through their words the Word has become flesh for us; through them we have access to the glory of God.

NOTES

Chapter 1: The Compulsion to Think
about Jesus Christ

1. The centrality of experience is perhaps all too casually assumed in contemporary culture, in part because experience is so readily equated with emotions, "feelings," valued so highly today. Sooner or later, however, most people become aware that feelings are tricky and even deceptive. Nevertheless, "experience" remains a necessary term in theology because there is an important noetic quality to it: Experience is "the apprehension of an object, thought, or emotion through the senses or mind" (*The American Heritage Dictionary* [2d college edition; Boston: Houghton Mifflin, 1982]). We can say that, theologically, experience is the apprehension of the object God by the person. Furthermore, this apprehension changes us in some way. It transforms our person because we interpret the object so apprehended as ultimately significant to our being. Rudolf Bultmann aptly calls this apprehension a new self-understanding (*Kerygma and Myth*, ed. H. W. Bartsch [New York: Macmillan Co., 1953], 202).

2. The ideas expressed here—and reflected in the entire perspective of the book—are informed by the sociology of knowledge. Important to me, as well as to many other New Testament scholars today, is the position of Peter L. Berger and Thomas Luckmann, *The Social Construction of Reality: A Treatise in the Sociology of Knowledge* (Garden City, N.Y.: Doubleday & Co., 1966).

3. For a fuller discussion, see pp. 42–43.

4. I agree entirely with the recent critique of the titles approach to Christology by Leander E. Keck, "Toward the Renewal of New Testament Christology," *New Testament Studies* 32 (1986): 368–70.

5. As Bultmann said years ago: "The saving efficacy of the cross is not derived from the fact that it is the cross of Christ; it is the cross of Christ because it has this saving efficacy." *Kerygma and Myth*, 41.

6. See the more detailed discussion in chap. 2, n. 7 below.

Chapter 2: God's Act of Restoration:
Justification by Grace

1. An accessible and detailed account will be found in Gunther Bornkamm, *Paul* (New York: Harper & Row, 1971).

2. The implication of current suggestions which find in Paul a detailed knowledge

of rhetorical practices is that Paul had more than a minimal knowledge of Hellenistic graduate education. An example here is H. D. Betz's commentary, *Galatians* (Hermeneia; Philadelphia: Fortress Press, 1979).

3. For brief discussions, see Leander Keck, *Paul and His Letters* (Philadelphia: Fortress Press, 1979), 3–4; Leander Keck and Victor Paul Furnish, *The Pauline Letters* (Nashville: Abingdon Press, 1984), 48–62.

4. See Albert Schweitzer, *The Mysticism of Paul the Apostle* (New York: Macmillan Co., 1955); Adolf Deissmann, *Paul: A Study in Social and Religious History* (London: Hodder & Stoughton, 1926); W. D. Davies, *Paul and Rabbinic Judaism* (4th ed.; Philadelphia: Fortress Press, 1980 repr.); more recently, E. P. Sanders, *Paul and Palestinian Judaism* (Philadelphia: Fortress Press, 1977); and J. Christiaan Beker, *Paul the Apostle: The Triumph of God in Life and Thought* (Philadelphia: Fortress Press, 1980).

5. Bultmann, *Theology of the New Testament* (New York: Charles Scribner's Sons, 1954); and Käsemann, perhaps best read in his *Commentary on Romans* (Grand Rapids: Wm. B. Eerdmans, 1980).

6. Emphasized by Ernst Käsemann, e.g., in *Perspectives on Paul* (Philadelphia: Fortress Press, 1971), 73.

7. Much is being said today about the contextualization of Paul's statements in his letters. This means that Paul was not writing abstract theological treatises but actual letters in which his primary concern was to relate to the churches and deal with their problems. In this sense we have Paul's "occasional" theology which he uses to deal with specific issues. This is to be granted as a beginning point. It is also to be granted that a reconstruction of a coherent theological structure is just that—reconstruction on the part of the interpreter.

But this in no way means that basic theological premises which lie behind the occasional statements cannot be legitimately discovered or inferred, or that reconstructions by interpreters are either invalid or inaccurate. To give up these enterprises is to give up one of the greatest tasks set before the interpreter—to recover the deep theological insight of the apostle—however imperfect even the most sensitive effort at reconstruction ultimately proves to be.

8. See my *Last Adam,* 59–112.

9. For my detailed wrestling with this issue, see "New Being: Renewed Mind: New Perception. Paul's View of the Source of Ethical Insight," *The Chicago Theological Seminary Register* 72 (1982): 1–12.

10. I again appeal to the insights of sociology of knowledge. See, e.g., Peter L. Berger and Thomas Luckmann, *The Social Construction of Reality: A Treatise in the Sociology of Knowledge* (Garden City, N.Y.: Doubleday & Co., 1966).

11. See the profound analysis of Rudolf Bultmann, "Romans 7 and the Anthropology of Paul," in *Existence and Faith,* ed. Schubert M. Ogden (Cleveland: World Pub., 1960), 147–57.

12. Of course a right relationship leads to genuine ethical performance. Paul is very clear about that.

13. E.g., H. J. Schoeps, *Paul: The Theology of the Apostle in the Light of Jewish*

Religious History (Philadelphia: Westminster Press, 1961), 213–18.

14. God as interpreted by the Pharisees and later rabbis is, of course, also loving. No one who has read the sources can doubt that there is a great struggle to emphasize God's love. Nor can one doubt that Paul must have known this topos. It does not, however, change his basic view of the internal dynamic which drives the system.

15. See the pungent observations of Krister Stendahl who has emphasized repeatedly that Paul was called, not converted: *Paul among Jews and Gentiles and Other Essays* (Philadelphia: Fortress Press, 1976), 7–23. This means that Paul did not see himself as founding a new religion. The churches were people loyal to Yahweh, and it is likely that the apostle saw them as part of the larger Jewish community.

16. Cf. my essay, "Paul as Rhetorician: Two Homilies in Romans 1—11," in *Jews, Greeks and Christians: Religious Cultures in Late Antiquity. Essays in Honor of William David Davies,* ed. Robert Hamerton-Kelly and Robin Scroggs (Leiden: E. J. Brill, 1976), 271–98.

17. E.g., Keck, *Paul and His Letters,* 78–81; J. Christiaan Beker, *Paul's Apocalyptic Gospel: The Coming Triumph of God* (Philadelphia: Fortress Press, 1982), 29–53.

18. It is fair to say that Paul sees through the "moral" God (a God of standards constructed by human views of what is acceptable and unacceptable) to the "covenantal" God whose purpose is to create a people true to God. When Paul says in Rom. 3:4, "Let God be true, [though] every person is false," (au. trans.), he is affirming God's covenant fidelity which he believes will ultimately be victorious (Romans 9—11) over all human attempts to thwart the establishment of a faithful covenant community.

19. An insight beautifully described by Richard L. Rubenstein, *My Brother Paul* (New York: Harper & Row, 1972), 11–13.

Chapter 3: The Cross: The Revelation
of the True World

1. A clear and succinct explanation of the Galatian situation can be found in Calvin J. Roetzel, *The Letters of Paul: Conversations in Context* (Atlanta: John Knox Press, 1975), 51–57.

2. For treatments of this perspective in early Christianity, see G. B. Caird, *Principalities and Powers* (Oxford: Clarendon Press, 1956); and Walter Wink, *Naming the Powers: The Language of Power in the New Testament* (Philadelphia: Fortress Press, 1984).

3. This hermeneutical principle is named the *gezerah shavah* by the rabbis and was much used by them, however artificial it may seem to our much-too-literal modern age. Paul uses the *gezerah shavah* also in Romans 4.

4. Bultmann has seen the similarity between Jewish pride in Torah and Greek striving for wisdom. See Rudolf Bultmann, *Theology of the New Testament* (New York: Charles Scribner's Sons, 1954), 1:240–41.

5. For Nietzsche's derivation of morality from resentment, see *The Genealogy of*

Morals (New York: Gordon Press, 1974). For his assault on Paul, see *The Antichrist* (Salem, N.H.: Ayer Co., 1972).

6. Paul's flexibility is not noted frequently enough, but this is an important dimension to his person: see, e.g., 1 Cor. 5:9; 9:19–23; Phil. 1:15–18; Rom. 14:1–15.

7. In Phil. 3:10–11 the chiastic form correlates fellowship in the sufferings of Christ with being conformed to his death. This may suggest Paul actually is thinking about the death of Jesus when he speaks of the sufferings of Christ.

8. On the identification of the opponents Paul writes against in 2 Corinthians, see the careful study of Victor Paul Furnish, *II Corinthians* (Anchor Bible; Garden City, N.Y.: Doubleday & Co., 1984), 52–54.

Chapter 4: The Victory of God in Christ

1. The issue is raised polemically by Käsemann in his paper, " 'The Righteousness of God' in Paul," in *New Testament Questions of Today* (Philadelphia: Fortress Press, 1969), 168–82. Bultmann's position can be studied at length in his *Theology of the New Testament* (New York: Charles Scribner's Sons, 1954), 1:270–330.

2. Best seen in Käsemann's *Commentary on Romans* (Grand Rapids: Wm. B. Eerdmans, 1980).

3. Scroggs, *Paul for a New Day,* 26.

4. Ibid., 59–60. For more detail, see Robin Scroggs, "New Being: Renewed Mind: New Perception. Paul's View of the Source of Ethical Insight," *The Chicago Theological Seminary Register* 72 (1982): 7–10.

5. Scroggs, *Paul for a New Day,* 29–37, 71–74.

6. See my "Paul as Rhetorician: Two Homilies in Romans 1—11," in *Jews, Greeks and Christians: Religious Cultures in Late Antiquity. Essays in Honor of William David Davies,* ed. Robert Hamerton-Kelly and Robin Scroggs (Leiden: E. J. Brill, 1976), 286–89.

7. See the discussion of this description of transformed existence in my "The Next Step: A Common Humanity," *Theology Today* 34 (1978): 395–401.

8. One should consult the commentaries on this difficult passage: e.g., Victor Paul Furnish, *II Corinthians* (Anchor Bible; Garden City, N.Y.: Doubleday & Co., 1984).

9. "The Lord is the Spirit" probably is an exegetical pointer to the meaning of "Lord" in Exod. 34:34. The "Spirit of the Lord" implies a close relationship—parallels can be found in Rom. 8:9 and Gal. 4:6. In 2 Cor. 3:18 both "Lord" and "Spirit" are in the genitive case. Grammatically there are three possibilities: the two words can be equated or either one given the priority (i.e., read "nominatively").

10. For an emphatic affirmation of future hope in Paul, see J. Christiaan Beker, *Paul's Apocalyptic Gospel: The Coming Triumph of God* (Philadelphia: Fortress Press, 1982), esp. 29–53.

11. The Epistle to the Hebrews reflects a somewhat similar theme in 7:25 and 9:24.

Chapter 5: Who Jesus Christ Was
and Is

1. I use the traditional term "person" to refer to discussion about "who Jesus was and is." For better or worse, the term "nature" also can be used more or less synonymously with "person" in such discussions, a use I have not been always able to avoid. In technical credal discussions, of course, "person" and "nature" are not synonymous. The reader will hopefully keep this ambiguity in terminology in mind through this chapter.

2. If this meaning is held to strictly, Paul accepts the idea that Jesus assumed sinful fleshly existence. It is also possible that he used the term "likeness" (*homoiōma*) to put some distance between the true humanity of Jesus and the actuality of his living in sinful flesh.

3. The word "spiritual" does mean, however, that the future eschatological humanity is noncorporeal. See my *Last Adam*, 65–68.

4. This conception of the power of the resurrected Christ to bestow his perfected existence on believers seems to be Paul's own unique contribution to first-century christological reflection.

5. Cf. above, pp. 39–40.

6. The three main passages are 1 Cor. 8:6; 2 Cor. 8:9; and Phil. 2:5–7. James D. G. Dunn challenges the usual interpretation of all of these passages and provides an alternative view in which no understanding of preexistence is necessary. See *Christology in the Making: A New Testament Inquiry into the Origins of the Doctrine of the Incarnation* (Philadelphia: Westminster Press, 1980), 114–23, 179–83. He has not convinced me.

7. The author of John certainly insists on the necessity of preexistence for his theological perspective. Cf. below, pp. 65–66.

8. It must be admitted, however, that for Paul Christ functions as the "mythological warrior" who fights in his enthroned lordship against the demonic powers, cf. 1 Cor. 15:24–26. This is not unlike the image of the warrior redeemer of *4 Ezra* 13:8–11, 32–38.

9. A relationship accepted by Hans Conzelmann, *An Outline of the Theology of the New Testament* (New York: Harper & Row, 1969), 73.

10. *4 Ezra* (c. 90–100 C.E.) has one reference to the death of the Messiah (7:29), but the authenticity of the text is uncertain. In Justin's *Dialogue with Trypho* the Jew Trypho says (or is made to say?) that he understood that the Messiah was to suffer but could not believe he would have such an ignominious death as crucifixion (chaps. 89—90). The Messiah ben Joseph, who is said to die, does not seem to have emerged in rabbinic discussions before the latter half of the second century C.E.

11. The reader can consult Oscar Cullmann, *The Christology of the New Testament* (Philadelphia: Westminster Press, 1959), 195–237.

12. The phrase "spirit of his Son" is unusual, but since, as we have seen, Paul's sense of the boundary between the act of Christ and that of the Spirit is fluid, the

apostle obviously felt no awkwardness in coining this expression. Betz may go too far in his judgment: "The Spirit 'of his son' in effect means the present reality of Christ," but the direction is certainly correct. See Hans Dieter Betz, *Galatians* (Hermeneia; Philadelphia: Fortress Press, 1979), 210.

13. See below, pp. 96–99.

14. Cullmann, *Christology*, 293.

15. For detailed treatment, see my *Last Adam*, 59–112.

16. R. H. Fuller, *The Foundations of New Testament Christology* (New York: Charles Scribner's Sons, 1965), 203–42.

Chapter 6: The Theological Setting of the Gospel of John

1. Questions about authorship, time and place of composition do not need to be raised here or standard answers repeated. The reader may consult commentaries. Especially convenient is the description of D. Moody Smith, *John* (Proclamation Commentaries, 2d ed., rev. and enl.; Philadelphia: Fortress Press, 1986), 72–81. "John" is a shorthand reference to the Gospel and the author; this does not suggest that some person named John is the author.

2. R. Alan Culpepper, *Anatomy of the Fourth Gospel: A Study in Literary Design* (Philadelphia: Fortress Press, 1983), 112. This book is an excellent introduction to the narrative approach to a Gospel.

3. For prominent discussions of the history of the Johannine community, see Raymond E. Brown, *The Community of the Beloved Disciple* (New York: Paulist Press, 1979); J. Louis Martyn, *History and Theology in the Fourth Gospel* (2d ed.; Nashville: Abingdon Press, 1979); and idem, *The Gospel of John in Christian History* (New York: Paulist Press, 1978), 90–121.

4. The Gnostic struggles for understanding are recorded in the documents from Nag Hammadi.

5. These statements assume the validity of sociologists of knowledge who speak about the world as social construction. For an introduction to this view, see Peter L. Berger and Thomas Luckmann, *The Social Construction of Reality: A Treatise in the Sociology of Knowledge* (Garden City, N.Y.: Doubleday & Co., 1966).

6. The author of the Gospel is not a philosopher or a religious scholar. Yet he shows awareness of many different strands of reflection current in the world of his day. One should consult the masterful study of C. H. Dodd, *The Interpretation of the Fourth Gospel* (Cambridge: Cambridge University Press, 1958).

7. For an overview, see Erwin R. Goodenough, *An Introduction to Philo Judaeus* (2d ed.; New York: Barnes & Noble, 1962), 91–160.

8. Obviously John did not invent this distinction, which is basic to the understanding of Israel and Judaism. He pushes the separation, however, about as far as is possible.

9. John thus refuses to give transcendent status to any dimension of humanity. With this he rejects Gnostic tendencies to see in humans, or some humans, a

"spark" of the divine. No one is of the godhead "by nature."

10. Marcion, the second-century Christian "heretic," split the godhead into two powers: the creator and the savior. The savior God and his Son have no relation to creation in any of its structures.

11. See Martyn, *History and Theology*.

12. The beautiful, so-called *Gospel of Truth*, despite its name, is also a nonnarrative tract and may have some historical relation with the later, more radical Johannine communities.

13. See the discussion in Smith, *John*, 82.

14. This perspective has now been strongly stated by Gail R. O'Day. In the conclusion of her analysis of the story of the Samaritan woman she writes: "John does not merely *present* the story of John 4 to the reader but instead narrates it in such a way that the reader *participates* in the narrative and the revelatory experience communicated by it" (*Revelation in the Fourth Gospel: Narrative Mode and Theological Claim* [Philadelphia: Fortress Press, 1986], 89, italics in original). She argues that this is true not only of that chapter but of the entire Gospel: "Revelation lies in the Gospel narrative and the world created by the words of that narrative!" p. 94, original in italics.

15. Bultmann's discussion is to be found in *Theology of the New Testament* (New York: Charles Scribner's Sons, 1955), 2:59–69, esp. 66.

16. I admit this is a very tricky statement. The very fact that John uses terms and symbols, taken from past religious traditions, as building blocks makes it inevitable that some content is being carried forward from the past, both in the author's mind and in the reader's. In the text of the Gospel, however, the author does not explicitly call attention to this past meaning. Bultmann suggests, more to the point of John's intention, that the tautology says something positive by the very fact of its denial of all human structures (*Theology* 2:67–69).

17. A strong statement affirming the reality of docetism in John's Christology is to be found in Ernst Käsemann, *The Testament of Jesus: A Study of the Gospel of John in the Light of Chapter 17* (Philadelphia: Fortress Press, 1968).

18. In addition to Culpepper's treatment of John as narrative (*Anatomy of the Fourth Gospel*), see Robert Kysar, *John's Story of Jesus* (Philadelphia: Fortress Press, 1984).

19. See n. 3 above.

20. See J. L. Houlden, *The Johannine Epistles* (New York: Harper & Row, 1973), 37–38; Raymond E. Brown, *The Epistles of John* (Anchor Bible; Garden City, N.Y.: Doubleday & Co., 1982), 19–30.

21. See Smith, *John*, 74.

Chapter 7: Unity with the Father

1. For an approach to the narrative of John, see Robert Kysar, *John's Story of Jesus* (Philadelphia: Fortress Press, 1984).

2. For a clear statement of this mode of interpretation, see J. Louis Martyn, *His-*

tory and Theology in the Fourth Gospel (2d ed.; Nashville: Abingdon Press, 1979), esp. 18–21.

3. Rudolf Bultmann titles this "The Revealer's farewell to his own" (*The Gospel of John: A Commentary* [Philadelphia: Westminster Press, 1971], 458). It is similar to "last testament" speeches such as those of Socrates in Plato's *Phaedo* and Paul in Acts 20:18–38.

4. See the exhaustive discussion in C. H. Dodd, *The Interpretation of the Fourth Gospel* (Cambridge: Cambridge University Press, 1958).

5. If v. 11 refers to events prior to the incarnation of the logos, this indicates the tension we described above, p. 59, in John's thought between the revelation in the Torah and that in the enfleshed logos. If, as Ernst Käsemann argues, v. 11 refers to the resistance offered to Jesus, then the tension is removed; see "The Structure and Purpose of the Prologue to John's Gospel," in *New Testament Questions of Today* (Philadelphia: Fortress Press, 1969), 144.

6. See Dodd, *Interpretation,* 170–76.

7. The intimacy which assures the validity of the revelation has already been stated in the climax of the prologue, v. 18, whether or not "God" or "Son" (as the RSV prefers) is the correct reading. One who is in the bosom of the Father is that "person" who knows in the most intimate fashion the reality and will of the Father. The reading, "Son," even if secondary is certainly consonant with Johannine Christology.

8. It should be repeatedly emphasized that John himself does not think substantively. Thus to know the Father means to know his act and will.

9. The common judgment, that Son of man is a title referring to a mythical savior figure in pre-Christian Jewish apocalyptic, has been seriously called into question. For a critical view, see Norman Perrin, *Rediscovering the Teaching of Jesus* (New York: Harper & Row, 1967), 164–73.

10. For other passages in which Jesus speaks of the Son of man, see John 6:27, 53, 62; 8:28.

11. This one exception is the long discourse in 5:16–29. Here all three sets of "Son" usages occur, along with a concentrated massing of the "Father" (9 times). As we will see in the following chapter, in this passage John is defending his Christology against the charge of ditheism.

12. On the "divine man" stratum visible in the Gospel, see Robert Fortna, *The Gospel of Signs* (Cambridge: Cambridge University Press, 1970), esp. 228–34. That signs are taken seriously by John is seen in the concluding statement of the original Gospel, which insists that the miracles of Jesus should lead to faith.

13. See the helpful summary in Robert Kysar, *John the Maverick Gospel* (Atlanta: John Knox Press, 1976), 40–44; also see the discussion in Bultmann, *John,* 225 n. 3.

14. Rudolf Bultmann, *Theology of the New Testament* (New York: Charles Scribner's Sons, 1955), 2:67–68. Bultmann says explicitly that John is not using the *via negativa,* which has the "ontological meaning of describing God's mode of being"

but is rather negating the world as a condemnation of humanity (p. 67). I find this a strange dichotomy. Granted, John does not say explicitly, "God is not this, not that"; the fact that he refuses to say what God is, however, seems to me to indicate his agreement with the intent of the *via negativa*.

15. As Bultmann correctly summarizes: "The death of Jesus is only rarely seen by him [the author of the Gospel] from the point of view of sacrifice, and in any case he nowhere else [than 1:29] attaches the gift of the forgiveness of sins specifically to Jesus' death, but understands it as the effect of his Word (8:31f)" (*John*, 96–97).

16. For a general overview of what the Greeks and Romans thought about the benevolence of divine powers, see Robert M. Grant, *Gods and the One God* (Philadelphia: Westminster Press, 1986), 54–123. The notion of divine *philanthropia* is found in Alexander, a second-century rhetorician, who uses the term in passing without definition or amplification. The passage is to be found in L. Spengel, *Rhetores Graeci* (Leipzig, 1856), 3:6.

17. See, e.g., J. L. Houlden, *Ethics and the New Testament* (New York: Oxford University Press, 1977), 35–41; Jack T. Sanders, *Ethics in the New Testament* (Philadelphia: Fortress Press, 1975; London: SCM Press, 1987), 91–100.

18. By this statement I do not mean to suggest that John solved the problem of theodicy any more than has anyone else. Nor does he deal with some of the sticky issues, assuming he even thought about them. His inclination toward a kind of predestination may reflect some struggle in his mind about the difficulties.

Chapter 8: Problems in John's Christology: Objections and Responses

1. For a comprehensive study of rabbinic judgments on the heretics who believed in "two powers," see Alan Segal, *Two Powers in Heaven: Early Rabbinic Reports about Christianity and Gnosticism* (Leiden: E. J. Brill, 1977).

2. See the discussion above, pp. 72–74, about the issue of glory, which conveys the same ambiguity as does that of miracles; and Robert Fortna, *The Gospel of Signs* (Cambridge: Cambridge University Press, 1970), 228–34.

3. For a careful statement of the importance and function of irony in John, see Gail R. O'Day, *Revelation in the Fourth Gospel: Narrative Mode and Theological Claim* (Philadelphia: Fortress Press, 1986). Paul D. Duke, *Irony in the Fourth Gospel* (Atlanta: John Knox Press, 1985), has a very helpful discussion of the passages reviewed in the text above; see esp. 63–82.

4. Wayne Meeks describes the problematic of the extreme but "inside" perspective of the Johannine claims as a reaction to the outside world; "The Man from Heaven in Johannine Sectarianism," *JBL* 91 (1972): 44–72 (reprinted in *The Interpretation of John* [ed. John Ashton; Philadelphia: Fortress Press; London: SPCK, 1986], 141–73).

5. Rudolf Bultmann, *Theology of the New Testament* (New York: Charles Scribner's Sons, 1955), 2:46.

Chapter 9: The Paraclete: The Light
Continues to Shine

1. See the interesting observations of Siegfried Schulz, *Untersuchungen zur Menschensohn Christologie im Johannesevangelium* (Göttingen: Vandenhoeck & Ruprecht, 1957), 142–51.

2. See, e.g., Robert Kysar, *John the Maverick Gospel* (Atlanta: John Knox Press, 1976), 93–95, and C. K. Barrett, *The Gospel according to St. John* (2d ed.; Philadelphia: Westminster Press, 1978), 462–63.

Chapter 10: The Work of Christ:
Believers and Unbelievers

1. John 5:28–29 presents a similar difficulty, apparently speaking of a future eschaton with judgment based on good deeds. This is especially a problem since it comes immediately after an affirmation of the presence of eternal life (5:25–27). Almost all scholars will affirm the primacy of present eschatology and attribute the future statements either to preservation of past tradition or to the hand of a later editor. See the discussion in Robert Kysar, *John the Maverick Gospel* (Atlanta: John Knox Press, 1976), 89–93.

2. Rudolf Bultmann, *The Gospel of John: A Commentary* (Philadelphia: Westminster Press, 1971), 159. I have mostly followed this translation in the quote but have changed a few words to bring out what I take to be the nuances of the original German, *Das Evangelium des Johannes* (Göttingen: Vandenhoeck & Ruprecht, 1964), 115.

3. Note, however, that what follows immediately are statements which speak of a future eschaton. See n. 1 above.

4. See above, p. 87.

5. Rudolf Bultmann, *Theology of the New Testament* (New York: Charles Scribner's Sons, 1955), e.g., 2:50, 67, 84–85.

6. I have been alerted by my colleague Professor Peter Van Ness that the word "participation" may have its own difficulties, in part because the term has technical meanings in Greek and Thomistic philosophy. I do not intend to import such technicalities into the discussion, but I admit that in my attempt to avoid difficulties in the term "mysticism," I may end up between a rock and a hard place.

7. For other passages, see 5:21; 6:39, 44; 10:29; 15:16, 19.

8. C. K. Barrett, *The Gospel according to St. John* (2d ed.; Philadelphia: Westminster Press, 1978), 502.

9. Bultmann, *Theology* 2:77.

10. How the struggle and defensiveness led to extreme theological assertions is well described by Wayne Meeks, "The Man from Heaven in Johannine Sectarianism," *Journal of Biblical Literature* 91 (1972): 44–72.

11. Ernst Haenchen, *John 2* (Hermeneia; Philadelphia: Fortress Press, 1984), 152.

Chapter 11: True God and True World:
Vision and Reality

1. For further reflections on the theological direction of Paul's Christology, see my "A Paul for Unitarian Universalists," *The Unitarian Universalist Christian* 41 (1986): 26–31.

SELECTED BIBLIOGRAPHY

Becker, J. C. *Paul the Apostle: The Triumph of God in Life and Thought.* Philadelphia: Fortress Press, 1980. An important book on Paul's theology, which stresses the centrality of apocalyptic in the apostle's thought.

Berger, P., and T. Luckmann. *The Social Construction of Reality: A Treatise in the Sociology of Knowledge.* Garden City, N.Y.: Doubleday & Co., 1966. A readable and insightful statement by two important sociologists, arguing that the world in which we live is created by societal values rather than ontological verities.

Bornkamm, G. *Paul.* New York: Harper & Row, 1971. Part I is an excellent description of what we can know about the historical Paul; Part II is an analysis of his theology.

Brown, Raymond E. *The Community of the Beloved Disciple.* New York: Paulist Press, 1979. An imaginative but careful reconstruction of the history of the Johannine community.

Bultmann, R. *Theology of the New Testament.* 2 vols. New York: Charles Scribner's Sons, 1955. One of the great works of the twentieth century, full of insights into both Paul and John.

Culpepper, A. *Anatomy of the Fourth Gospel: A Study in Literary Design.* Philadelphia: Fortress Press, 1983. The most detailed treatment of the Gospel from the standpoint of narrative criticism.

Davies, W. D. *Paul and Rabbinic Judaism.* 4th ed. Philadelphia: Fortress Press, 1980 [1948]. A comprehensive treatment of Paul from the standpoint of his Jewish background.

Käsemann, E. *Perspectives on Paul.* Philadelphia: Fortress Press, 1971. An exciting and pungent interpretation of Paul's theology from the perspective of a radicalized Lutheran theology.

————. *The Testament of Jesus: A Study of the Gospel of John in the Light of Chapter 17.* Philadelphia: Fortress Press, 1968. A provocative interpretation of the Gospel.

Keck, L. *Paul and His Letters.* Proclamation Commentaries. Philadelphia: Fortress Press, 1979. A helpful and succinct treatment of the apostle and his writings.

Keck, L., and V. Furnish. *The Pauline Letters.* Nashville: Abingdon Press, 1984. A balanced and up-to-date treatment of the Pauline corpus.

Kysar, R. *John: The Maverick Gospel.* Atlanta: John Knox Press, 1976. Perhaps the best nontechnical introduction to the Gospel.

———. *John's Story of Jesus*. Philadelphia: Fortress Press, 1984. A telling of the story from the perspective of John's plot.

Martyn, L. *History and Theology in the Fourth Gospel*. 2d ed. Nashville: Abingdon Press, 1979. An insightful study of the relations between the Johannine church and the synagogue, showing that this conflict sets much of the tone for the Gospel stories.

Roetzel, C. *The Letters of Paul: Conversations in Context*. Atlanta: John Knox Press, 1975. A helpful introduction to the Pauline letters, explaining the situations which Paul is addressing.

Scroggs, R. *The Last Adam: A Study in Pauline Anthropology*. Philadelphia: Fortress Press, 1966. A study of Paul's views of Christ and the transformed person as informed by Jewish ideas of Adam.

———. *Paul for a New Day*. Philadelphia: Fortress Press, 1976. A brief, general treatment of Paul's theology.

Smith, D. M. *John*. Proclamation Commentaries. 2d ed., rev. and enl. Philadelphia: Fortress Press, 1986. A very helpful introduction to the complexities of the Gospel.

Stendahl, K. *Paul among Jews and Gentiles and other Essays*. Philadelphia: Fortress Press, 1976. A minor classic which outlines helpful new ways of thinking about the apostle.